T0363844

OPEN WORLD

B1
PRELIMINARY

WORKBOOK
WITHOUT
ANSWERS

with Audio Download

Sheila Dignen

with Sarah Dymond

Cambridge University Press
www.cambridge.org/elt

Cambridge Assessment English
www.cambridgeenglish.org

Information on this title: www.cambridge.org/9781108565370

© Cambridge University Press & Assessment and UCLES 2019

This publication is in copyright. Subject to statutory exception
and to the provisions of relevant collective licensing agreements,
no reproduction of any part may take place without the written
permission of Cambridge University Press.

First published 2019

20 19 18 17 16 15 14

Printed in Poland by Opolgraf

A catalogue record for this publication is available from the British Library

ISBN   978-1-108-56537-0   Workbook without answers with Audio Download

The publishers have no responsibility for the persistence or accuracy
of URLs for external or third-party internet websites referred to in this publication,
and do not guarantee that any content on such websites is, or will remain,
accurate or appropriate. Information regarding prices, travel timetables, and other
factual information given in this work is correct at the time of first printing but
the publishers do not guarantee the accuracy of such information thereafter.

CONTENTS

S PERSONAL PROFILE

VOCABULARY

1 Write the words for the personal interests.

1

m _____ _____ _____ c

2

t _____ _____ _____ _____ l

3

f _____ _____ _____ _____ _____ n

4

c _____ _____ _____ _____ g

5

s _____ _____ _____ _____ s

6

a _____ _____ s and
c _____ _____ _____ _____ s

2 Complete the sentences with the correct form of the verbs in the box.

| buy | cook | learn | listen | make | play |

1 I like _____ to music.

2 My brother enjoys _____ football and other sports.

3 Elsie loves _____ new clothes – that's why she never has any money!

4 I enjoy _____ meals for my family.

5 My sister likes _____ things, so she does a lot of arts and crafts.

6 I love _____ about different fashions in the past.

3 Choose the correct words to complete the text.

During the week, I usually get ¹*up / out / in* quite early, then I ²*do / have / make* a shower and get dressed. I ³*do / go / have* breakfast at about 7.30, and then I pick up my bag and ⁴*leave / get / go* to college. I have classes all morning, then I ⁵*take / have / go* lunch with my friends before the afternoon classes. I don't usually meet ⁶*up / out / to* with my friends in the evenings, because I have a part-time job as a waiter. When I'm not working, I like keeping fit, so I often work ⁷*up / out / off* at the gym. At the weekends, I often hang ⁸*up / off / out* with my friends. We sometimes eat ⁹*up / out / over*, but not too often because it's quite expensive.

4 Read the clues that people give about their occupations. Write the occupations.

1 I enjoy helping customers choose the right things to buy.
I'm a s_____ a_____.

2 I love food and cooking, so this is my dream job!
I'm a c_____.

3 My job is important to help people know what's happening in the world.
I'm a j_____.

4 I love working outside, and it's great when I see my plants growing.
I'm a g_____.

5 Without me, there would be a lot more crime.
I'm a p_____ o_____.

6 You come to me if you have a problem with your car.
I'm a m_____.

7 I love chatting to people while I make their hair look amazing.
I'm a h_____.

GRAMMAR

1 Complete the sentences with the present simple or present continuous form of the verbs in brackets. Remember to think about the position of the adverbs of frequency.

1 My brother _____ (never / get up) early!

2 Mmm, I _____ (enjoy) this soup – it's lovely!

3 Bankers _____ (usually / earn) a lot of money.

4 My sister _____ (always / borrow) my clothes without asking. It's so annoying!

5 More people _____ (become) vegetarians now.

6 Hollywood films _____ (often / be) really exciting.

7 I _____ (not / read) a book at the moment. Can you recommend one?

8 Tim _____ (not like) cooking.

9 My dad _____ (always / tell) really bad jokes in front of my friends. It's so embarrassing!

10 Jack _____ (not work) as a gardener at the moment.

2 Complete the questions with the question words in the box and then match them to the answers a–f.

> how   what   when   where   who   why

1 _____ do you live?
2 _____ do you hang out with at the weekend?
3 _____ are your exams?
4 _____ old are you?
5 _____ do you do on Saturdays?
6 _____ are you happy today?

a With my friends.
b Because it's the weekend!
c I often go shopping.
d I live in London.
e They're next month.
f I'm nineteen.

3 Write the words in the correct order to make questions.

1 you / doing / what / are
_____?

2 what time / film / start / does / the
_____?

3 who / Max / is / to / talking
_____?

4 home / going / now / they / are
_____?

5 Sam / restaurant / work / in / does / a
_____?

6 what / usually / have / you / do / for breakfast
_____?

4 Complete the posts with the correct verb forms.

What do you love and hate about Mondays?

JayT44
At the moment I ¹_____ (study) to be a doctor. Mondays are difficult for me because I ²_____ (usually / be) tired after the weekend! Why ³_____ (the weekends / go) so quickly?

EllieZZ
I ⁴_____ (go / sometimes) away with friends for the weekend. It's great, except my friend Anna ⁵_____ (always / borrow) my clothes and make-up – it's really annoying when I can't find something I need for work on Monday morning!

Joe99
I'm a student, and on Mondays I ⁶_____ (have) a really difficult maths class. I have to study maths because I ⁷_____ (train) to be a mechanic, but I ⁸_____ (hate) it!

LISTENING

1 🎧 02 Listen to three young people talking about their jobs and daily routines. Choose the job that each person does or wants to do.

1 Maria
  restaurant chef / cookery vlogger / food writer
2 Sam
  teacher / sports photographer / tennis player
3 Anika
  journalist / police officer / doctor

2 🎧 02 Listen again and write M (Maria), S (Sam) or A (Anika).

Which person …?
1 doesn't want to work in the evenings _____
2 is working and also studying _____
3 doesn't often eat out _____
4 is interested in music _____
5 wants to travel in the future _____
6 meets different people as part of their job _____

3 🎧 03 Complete the sentences with one word in each gap. Listen and check.

1 I'm really interested _____ food.
2 I don't want to work _____ a chef in a restaurant.
3 I'm winning quite a lot of games _____ the moment.
4 I also listen _____ music a lot at home.
5 I also work _____ a newspaper in my town.
6 This is the right job _____ me.

READING

1 Read an interview with Tom, a British man who is working as a ninja in Japan. Match questions a–g with gaps 1–6. There is one question you don't need.

a Is it difficult to become a ninja?

b What is a ninja?

c Is there anything you don't like about the job?

d What's your daily routine like?

e What special clothes do ninjas wear?

f What do you enjoy the most about your job?

g What does a professional ninja do nowadays?

(1) _____

Ninjas are traditional fighters in Japan. They usually fight using their hands. They also use high jumps and kicks, so they're very fit. There aren't any real ninjas now, but people still learn the skills because ninjas are important in Japanese culture.

(2) _____

Some towns and cities in Japan employ ninjas because tourists like them. The ninjas put on shows of their skills in the streets. They also talk to tourists about the ninja traditions. Tourists also love taking photos of themselves with a ninja!

(3) _____

Yes, it is. You have to be very fit, and you have to practise a lot to learn all the skills. You also need a good memory, because you need to learn about the history of ninjas and why they're important in Japanese culture.

(4) _____

I get up early and have a light breakfast. Then I practise my skills for two hours. I often practise with other ninjas, which is fun. Then at 10.30 I start work in the city centre. We do four or five shows a day, so it's quite tiring. Then in the evenings I usually work out for an hour, because you need to be strong to be a ninja. So there isn't much time for hanging out with friends!

(5) _____

Everything! I really like learning the ninja skills. You feel so good when you manage to do something new. At the moment I'm trying to learn a really difficult move, and I love that challenge. I also enjoy talking to the tourists, especially the kids. They're funny because they always want to fight me!

(6) _____

Yes, I hate the fact that I can't have chips or chocolate! Ninjas have to be small and not very heavy, so I'm very careful about what I eat. But it's worth it so I can do a job that I love.

2 Read the text again. Decide if the sentences are true or false.

1 There are still a few real ninjas in Japan.

2 Modern ninjas work to entertain tourists.

3 You have to learn skills and study to become a ninja.

4 Tom spends a lot of time relaxing with friends.

5 Tom finds children annoying when he's working.

6 Tom can't eat all the things he would like to eat.

3 Match the highlighted words and phrases in the text with the meanings.

1 I get something from it, even though it's difficult. _____

2 give someone a job _____

3 with not much food _____

4 belonging to the past and the culture of a country _____

5 something that is difficult to do or learn _____

6 the way of life and beliefs that the people of a country share _____

SPEAKING

1 Write the words in the correct order to make expressions for starting a conversation and keeping it going.

1 name / what's / your

_____?

2 meet / nice / you / to

_____.

3 from / you / where / are

_____?

4 you / do / what / do

_____?

5 you / are / how

_____?

6 like / you / to / music / listening / do

_____?

2 Match the answers with the questions and expressions in exercise 1.

a New York. It's a great city! _____

b It's Paul. _____

c Yes, I do. I love it! _____

d I'm fine, thanks. _____

e I'm a journalist. _____

f Nice to meet you, too. _____

3 Choose the correct responses.

1 I go running three times a week.
 A I agree. I like running, too.
 B Really? I like running, too.

2 Hi. My name's George.
 A Nice to meet you.
 B How are you?

3 I love cooking.
 A I am too.
 B Me too.

4 I'm a chef.
 A That sounds interesting.
 B I agree. Do you work in a restaurant?

5 I think the job of a police officer is very difficult.
 A Really? And it's dangerous, too.
 B I agree. It's quite dangerous, too.

6 I work in London.
 A Really? What do you do?
 B That sounds interesting. How are you?

WRITING

1 Complete the blog entry with the correct words and phrases (a–g).

Hello! **1**_____ and I'm 22. I'm Spanish and I live in Madrid. **2**_____ and I work for a big computer company. **3**_____!
I usually get up at seven o'clock **4**_____. I get home at about seven in the evening **5**_____. Then I usually watch TV before I go to bed.
I love sport, especially football. **6**_____ and I also love watching sport on TV. **7**_____. I can make really good pizzas!

a and I start work at eight

b I play for a team in my town

c My name's Alejandro

d I also enjoy cooking

e and I prepare some food

f I'm a computer programmer

g Welcome to my blog

2 Read the first part of another blog entry. Find and correct six mistakes.

Hello! My name's Rob and I'm 18 year old. At the moment I'm study to become police officer. Welcome to my blog!
My classes start usually at nine o'clock, so I always get up early. I always am tired when I get home in the evenings. At the weekend I enjoy hang out with my friends, and we often go to the cinema together.

1 GETTING AWAY

VOCABULARY

1 Match the beginnings and ends of the sentences that Sofia says about her holiday activities.

1 I always feel excited when I'm packing ____
2 I love discovering ____
3 I don't spend much time just sunbathing by ____
4 I don't buy ____
5 I always take ____
6 I like hiking ____
7 It's nice to spend a day sightseeing ____
8 I always have fun playing ____
9 When I go to a new city, I prefer exploring on ____

a many souvenirs to take home with me.
b exciting new places when I'm on holiday.
c the pool or on the beach.
d games on the beach with friends.
e in the mountains if the weather's nice.
f lots of photos!
g my own, rather than going on a tour.
h in a new city and visiting all the tourist sites.
i my bags to go on holiday.

2 Choose the correct words to complete the sentences.

1 I think going on a long ____ by train would be really boring!
   A transport   B journey   C travel
2 We're going on a ten-day ____ to Morocco next month.
   A trip   B travel   C transport
3 Flying is not always the most expensive form of ____.
   A tour   B transport   C trip
4 We went on a ____ of the old city with a really interesting guide.
   A trip   B journey   C tour
5 I'd love to do a job that involves a lot of ____.
   A travel   B transport   C journey

3 Complete the sentences with the correct weather words.

1 It's quite c ____ today, so you might need a sweatshirt.
2 I hate it when the weather's grey and d ____ !
3 What's the c ____ m ____ e like where you live?
4 I hate it when it rains and everything feels d ____ p.
5 There was a storm last night, with lots of thunder and l ____ t ____ g.
6 It's warm here during the day, but it can be quite c ____ y in the evening.

4 Choose the correct words to complete the online posts.

JJ44
I'm looking for somewhere to go on a hiking holiday in November. Any suggestions?

Marty_P
The island of Madeira is nice at that time of year. It's quite warm, with blue skies and plenty of ¹*sunshine / showers / climate*. It's a nice dry heat, too, so it doesn't feel too ²*dull / humid / mild*. Perfect!

SammyT33
I went to the Caribbean last year, but I wouldn't recommend it in November. It's the beginning of the wet season, so there may be frequent heavy ³*chilly / showers / damp*. It's also windy at that time of year too, so there may be a strong ⁴*lightning / breeze / dull*.

Suzy_S21
Why not go to Tenerife? It doesn't often rain there, so you can be fairly sure you'll get ⁵*fine / dull / damp* weather. Nights can be ⁶*mild / chilly / humid*, though, so take a few warm clothes with you.

GRAMMAR

1 Complete the advice about booking a holiday with the correct comparative or superlative form of the adjectives.

Booking a holiday?

Price isn't everything when you're booking a holiday, and the ¹____ (cheap) holiday isn't necessarily the ²____ (good) one. For example, one hotel may cost less than another, but it may be a long way from the airport, so it's ³____ (expensive) to get there by taxi. Also, a hotel that has low prices might have a ⁴____ (small) pool than other hotels. This probably means the pool will be ⁵____ (crowded) and not much fun! Many people choose the ⁶____ (big) hotel they can find because they think this will have the ⁷____ (comfortable) rooms. But this isn't always true, and big hotels are often ⁸____ (noisy) than small ones. So, when you're looking for a holiday, don't just think about price – think about which holiday will be the ⁹____ (enjoyable) for you.

8

2 Complete the second sentence so it has a similar meaning to the first. Use *less ...* or *(not) as ... .*

1 This hotel is older than the one near the beach.
The hotel near the beach _____isn't as old_____ as this one

2 The beach was more crowded yesterday.
The beach is _____ today than it was yesterday.

3 This café is less expensive than the Italian one.
This café _____ as the Italian one.

4 This beach is beautiful, and the one we went to yesterday was beautiful too.
This beach is as _____ the one we went to yesterday.

5 This city isn't as interesting as I expected.
This city _____ than I expected.

3 Complete the holiday complaints with *too* or *enough* and the words in brackets.

1 The pool was _____ (cold) to swim in!

2 I guess our room was _____ (clean), but it wasn't nicely decorated.

3 There were lots of restaurants, but they were all _____ (expensive) for us.

4 Our balcony wasn't _____ (big) for us to sit on.

5 We only stayed for a few days, so we didn't have _____ (time) to do very much.

4 Complete the sentences with *so* or *such a*.

1 I'm _____ happy that I'm going on holiday tomorrow!

2 Why have you got _____ big bag?

3 Spain is _____ lovely country to visit!

4 It was _____ exciting going on the boat trip.

5 I'd love to go to Cuba, but it's _____ long way!

5 Choose the correct words to complete the email.

Hi Paula,

I'm having ¹*so / such / enough* a great time here in Ireland. The countryside is even ²*more / the most / as* beautiful than I expected, and the people here are ³*enough / such / so* friendly and welcoming. It isn't ⁴*less hot / hotter / as hot as* Spain, of course, but it's ⁵*too warm / so warm / warm enough* for hiking and sightseeing. Luckily, it hasn't been ⁶*such / more / too* wet – we've only had one day of rain! The ⁷*more / most / less* surprising thing is the food – it's amazing, and it's ⁸*so / less / as* expensive than I thought, which is good! The ⁹*bigger / too big / biggest* problem has been travelling around. The buses here are ¹⁰*cheaper / so cheap / not as cheap* than the trains, but there aren't many of them in the countryside, so I think we might need to hire a car.

See you when I get back,
Jan

Complete the words in the sentences.

1 Some parts of the world are getting much warmer because of c_____ m_____ e c_____ge.

2 Plastic water bottles are definitely not e_____ r_____ m_____ t_____ y f_____ n_____ y!

3 Travelling by train rather than plane will reduce your c_____ b_____ n f_____ t_____ t.

4 We all need to recycle more so that we produce less w_____ e.

5 We should use clean forms of energy rather than burning f_____ s_____ l f_____ s.

6 It's important to support the c_____ s_____ v_____ n of the rainforest.

LISTENING

1 04 **Listen to an interview on a holiday show. What is the show about?**

A an unusual holiday on a cruise ship that costs a lot of money

B a competition in which someone can win a luxury holiday

C a holiday company that wants to pay someone to go on holiday

2 04 **Listen to the interview again. Decide if the sentences are true or false.**

1 The company wants someone to go on seven different holidays.

2 The person has to write a blog and upload photos to social media.

3 The person also has to upload a video, but they can't choose what it is about.

4 The person won't pay for their travel or food, and will also receive money to pay for souvenirs.

5 The company is employing this person to help advertise its holidays.

6 To apply, you should write to the company and send some of your holiday photos.

For each question, choose the correct answer.

The people below all want to find a hotel near the beach. On the right there are eight hotels near the beach. Decide which hotel would be most suitable for the people below.

1 Tanya wants a hotel directly on the beach so she can go for long walks. Apart from that, she doesn't plan to leave her hotel, so wants all meals and plenty of things to do there.

2 Susie wants to stay at a small quiet hotel. She wants the hotel to provide transport to a nearby town so that she can do lots of shopping there.

3 Rafael needs a hotel which provides suitable activities and food for young children. He also wants the hotel restaurant to serve a range of international food that he and his wife can enjoy.

4 Tommy is looking for a hotel with access to a gym and swimming pool. He also wants his hotel to be within walking distance of entertainment facilities for the evenings.

5 Angelica and her sister Katrin want a hotel which is next to a busy beach where they can take lessons in a watersport and go swimming in the sea.

HOLIDAY HOTELS

A LUXUS HOTEL
You never need to step outside this hotel as it has a full programme of activities for adults, from fitness classes and yoga to cooking lessons and garden tours. There's also a choice of four international restaurants to suit different tastes. The balcony has fantastic views over the town and the beach beyond.

B OCEAN VIEW
It's easy to visit the local attractions – a castle and a children's fun park – because the public bus stops outside the hotel entrance. Behind the hotel is a small beach which is often crowded with sunbathers and swimmers. There's also a diving and sailing school, where hotel guests can get a discount.

C SEASIDE HOTEL
This small, family-owned hotel offers fantastic home-cooked food. The hotel is only five minutes' walk to a busy beach but it's outside a town. If guests wish to go out in the evenings, it's better to bring your own car or hire one.

D GOLDEN SANDS HOTEL
This friendly hotel has a fantastic sports and entertainment programme to keep kids busy all day. There's only one restaurant but the menu changes daily, includes food from around the world and is suitable for all ages. There's an evening babysitting service so that adults can eat later.

E BLUE WAVES HOTEL
This busy hotel is ten minutes on foot to the town where there are discos and nightly concerts. The fitness centre's great for those who want to stay active on holiday, and guests can use the twenty-five-metre pool at the hotel next door. Free transport is provided to and from the airport.

F HARRY'S HOTEL
This hotel is right on the beach so guests can sit and watch surfers in the water. There are only twenty-five bedrooms so the atmosphere's always peaceful. All meals are provided and are cooked by a French chef. The town centre's great for buying gifts, clothes and shoes, and the hotel minibus takes guests there for free.

G DUNES HOTEL
This hotel, located away from the town, has everything you need, from a large swimming pool, games room and gym to clothes shops and a mini-supermarket. Breakfast and dinner are included, and it's possible to add lunch for a small charge. To reach the five-kilometre sandy beach, guests just need to cross the hotel garden.

H SUNSET HOTEL
A ten-minute taxi ride along the coast takes guests to a nearby town with a choice of watersports, including surfing and windsurfing lessons, as well as lively nightlife. The hotel has a private beach for sunbathing, but for swimming it's best to use the hotel pool.

1 Read the phrases. Decide if each one is making a suggestion (S), asking for an opinion (O), agreeing (A) or disagreeing (D).

1 What do you think? ....

2 Sorry, but I don't agree. ....

3 Yes, you're right. ....

4 Perhaps they could visit a museum. ....

5 That's true. ....

6 Do you agree? ....

7 I think they should go to the beach. ....

8 Really? ....

2 Complete the conversations with the words in the box. There are two words you don't need.

afraid	agree	best	enjoy	great
might	opinion	really	think	

A: They ¹............ like a trip to the theatre.

B: Do you ²............ so? I'm not sure.

A: I think the ³............ way to get to Paris is by train.

B: I'm ⁴............ I disagree with you. The train is too slow.

A: I think they'd ⁵............ going shopping. What's your ⁶............ ?

B: I think that's a ⁷............ idea. Most people like shopping.

3 Choose the correct phrases in the conversations.

A: ¹Perhaps they could / They might like spend the day sightseeing.

B: ²That's true. / Really? I think that might be fun.

A: ³I think they'd enjoy / I think they should visiting the zoo.

B: ⁴Do you agree? / Yes, you're right. They'd like that.

A: I think a barbecue is the best idea for a meal. ⁵What do you think? / Really?

B: ⁶I'm afraid I disagree with you. / Yes, you're right. A barbecue isn't fun if it's raining.

4 Choose the best answer to each question.

1 Do you prefer to travel by plane or by train?

A I'd rather go by plane because it's quicker.

B Trains and planes are both expensive, but the train is usually a bit cheaper.

2 What do you think about organised tours?

A I sometimes go on organised tours, but I usually explore new cities on my own.

B I think organised tours can be interesting sometimes, if you're in a new city.

3 Would you rather spend a day sunbathing or sightseeing?

A I love sunbathing, and I also like sightseeing because it's interesting.

B I'd prefer to go sightseeing for the day because I think it's more interesting.

4 What's the best time of year for you to go on holiday?

A I think the spring is my favourite time to go on holiday because it isn't as busy as the summer.

B The summer is usually too expensive for some people, so a lot of people prefer the autumn.

5 Do you enjoy hiking in the mountains?

A There are lots of great mountains in my country, and a lot of people go hiking there.

B Yes, I love hiking in the mountains because you can get some amazing views from the top.

1 Choose the correct linking words.

1 *Although / But* the beach was crowded, there was enough space for us to find a place to relax.

2 The city centre has some beautiful old buildings. *What's more, / As well*, there are also some amazing shops.

3 The hotel has two swimming pools, and tennis courts *also / too*.

4 The food was excellent, *and / but* the waiters were all very friendly.

5 *As well as / Also* visiting the museum, we also had time for lunch in a small café.

6 The train journey was long, *what's more / but* we didn't mind because the scenery was beautiful.

2 Complete the sentences with the linking words in the box.

also	although
and	as well as
though	too

1 A helicopter trip is a great way to see the city, ... it doesn't cost too much.

2 The old city centre is lovely, and the castle is .... worth a visit.

3 .... we were tired, we decided to go for a walk along the beach.

4 .... being very crowded, the museum was old-fashioned and not very interesting.

5 The park is a great place to relax. There's a very good café there, ...

6 We had an amazing holiday. It was very expensive, ...

2 ENTERTAIN ME

VOCABULARY

Read the clues and complete the puzzle with the correct entertainment words. Use the shaded letters to make an extra word.

1	S			D	T				
2	B			S				R	
3	A					E			
4	T					R			
5	E		S						
6	C								
7	S								

1 the music that plays during a film
2 a very popular book that a lot of people buy
3 the people who watch a play or show
4 a very exciting film or book
5 one part of a TV series
6 a funny film that makes you laugh
7 the part of a theatre where the actors stand to perform

Extra word: d ....

Clue: It might be about animals.

GRAMMAR

1 Complete the text with the present perfect or past simple form of the verbs.

Nearly a star!

Do you want to be a star? I **¹** .... (never / be) interested in being on TV, but last year a friend of mine **²** .... (go) to an event to find good singers for a talent show. He **³** .... (always / love) singing, so it **⁴** .... (seem) perfect for him. He **⁵** .... (sing) well for the judges, and they **⁶** .... (accept) him onto the show. He's really excited because he **⁷** .... (not do) anything like this before. As for me, I **⁸** .... (never / see) a friend of mine on TV before, so I can't wait to watch the show!

2 Write the questions using the present perfect or past simple form of the verbs. Then complete the short answers.

1 A: you / enjoy / the concert / last Saturday?

.... ?

   B: Yes, I .... It was amazing!

2 A: you / ever / act / in a play?

.... ?

   B: Yes, I .... But I don't think I was very good!

3 A: you / go / to / any festivals / last summer?

.... ?

   B: No, I .... But I'd like to go to some this year.

4 A: Paul / see / the new *Star Wars* film yet?

.... ?

   B: Yes, he .... He loved it!

5 A: Freya / win / the singing competition / last week?

.... ?

   B: Yes, she .... She's a really good singer!

6 A: your friends / ever / organise / a surprise party for you?

.... ?

   B: No, they .... , but I organised one for a friend of mine recently.

3 Complete the second sentence so it has the same meaning as the first. Use *for* or *since*.

1 I started at this college in 2019.
I've been at this _____ 2019.

2 Ollie started work at the café three months ago.
Ollie has worked at _____ three months.

3 My brother got this tablet last year.
My brother has had this _____ last year.

4 I first met Laura five years ago.
I've known _____ five years.

5 Hana became interested in dance when she was five.
Hana has been interested _____ she was five.

6 My grandparents started living in this house a long time ago.
My grandparents have lived in _____ a long time.

4 Complete the conversation with *yet* and *already*.

A: Have you seen the latest episode of *Secret Lives* ¹ _____?

B: No, I haven't. I know it's on catch-up TV, but I haven't had time to watch it ² _____.
But I've ³ _____ decided that it was David who killed Magda.

A: Really? I think there are a few possibilities.

B: Yes, but the police have ⁴ _____ found a few things that show it's David.

A: Hmm, but they haven't arrested him ⁵ _____, so I'm not sure. Freddie says there are some spoilers online – have you read any of them ⁶ _____?

B: No, and I don't want to – I'm happy to wait and see what happens!

5 Complete the text with the correct form of *used to* and the verbs in brackets.

In the early days of film-making things
¹ _____ (be) very different for the actors. Firstly, they ² _____
(not speak) in the films, because there was no sound. Someone ³ _____ (play) the piano in cinemas while the audience watched the film. And how ⁴ _____
(they / do) dangerous things, like in this photo?
Nowadays, film makers can use computers to make things look exciting, or they use special actors to do the dangerous scenes. But in the 1920s that ⁵ _____
(not happen). The main actors ⁶ _____
_____ (perform) in every scene, even when it was dangerous!

 For each question, choose the correct answer.

1 You will hear two friends talking about a film they have just seen.
What does the woman say?
A The film was too long.
B The story was hard to follow.
C The main actor was disappointing.

2 You will hear a brother and sister talking about booking concert tickets.
They agree to book seats
A near the stage.
B at the side.
C in the balcony.

3 You will hear a woman telling a friend about a TV programme.
What type of programme did she watch?
A a soap opera
B a crime series
C a documentary

4 You will hear two people talking about online newspapers.
Why does the man prefer online newspapers to TV news?
A They are more suitable for his busy lifestyle.
B They focus on more interesting topics.
C They provide more detailed information.

5 You will hear a man telling a friend about a play called *The Visit*.
How does he feel?
A satisfied that he has seen it
B impressed by the way that it ended
C excited about the director's next play

6 You will hear two friends talking about a summer music festival.
One thing the woman likes about the festival is that
A it isn't too crowded.
B tickets aren't too expensive.
C travelling there isn't too difficult.

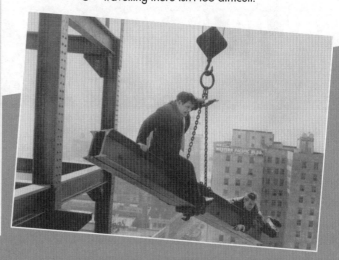

1 Read the article. How does it answer the question in the title below? Choose the best answer.

A Not many people knew about superheroes in the past, but now more people know about them.

B The use of computers has made superhero films more realistic, so now more people can enjoy them.

C Film makers now use better stories in superhero films, so they are more exciting.

Everyone is suddenly crazy about superhero films! Recent films like *Black Panther*, *The Avengers* and *Thor* have become popular all over the world. But why? Most of the characters are not new. They have been in stories in comics since the 1960s. So why are superhero films suddenly so popular now?

One reason is that the basic superhero story is very simple and familiar. We would all love to be a superhero – a normal person who gets amazing magic powers. We can imagine that suddenly we are super-strong or can run super-fast, or fly through the air. We then use these powers to fight a bad guy who wants to destroy the world, and everyone loves us! Wonderful!

These stories worked well in comics. Artists made simple drawings of Spiderman climbing up walls or Superman flying above the city. Our imagination did the rest. But with superhero films in the past, this didn't work. The audience couldn't believe the story they were watching. They could see that the superheroes weren't *really* flying, or climbing up walls. They just looked like normal people in rather silly clothes!

But this has all changed. Budgets are much bigger and films are much better than they used to be. The costumes actors wear now are amazing. But there's something more important. Film makers now use computers to make the superheroes *look* real. When we see Superman flying, we can now *believe* that he is flying.

Because the stories now *look* real on the screen, we can enjoy them again, like we did in the comics. Our imagination can take control again. We can believe there really *is* a superhero, and he (or she) really *can* save the world! At the same time, we can enjoy the amazing pictures, the soundtrack and the excellent acting.

Fans have waited for a long time to see good superhero films. But they are finally here. Now not just children, but old and young alike, can escape into these imaginary worlds. With the help of computers and amazing special effects, everyone can really enjoy these simple stories of magic and power, and good defeating bad.

WHY DO WE SUDDENLY LOVE SUPERHEROES?

2 Read the article again. Choose the correct answers.

1 Most of the characters in superhero films *have changed / haven't changed* since the 1960s.

2 Most people *can imagine they are / wouldn't like to* be a superhero.

3 Audiences thought the first film superheroes were *amazing / looked disappointing*.

4 It is easier to enjoy superhero films now because *they look more like the stories in comics / they look more realistic*.

5 *Especially young people / People of all ages* now enjoy superhero films.

Choose the correct phrasal verbs to complete the sentences.

1 I used to be good friends with Ali, but I _____ with him last year.
2 My brother has really _____ tennis recently – he loves it!
3 You shouldn't worry about things so much – you should _____ more!
4 Henry was really upset when his band _____ last year.
5 I think if you enjoy acting, you should _____ doing it – don't listen to anyone else!
6 My parents always want me to do well, and I don't want to _____.
7 A local café offered me a part-time job, but I _____.
8 Ben's dad is a famous actor, so Ben feels he has to _____.

	A	B	C
1	**A** fell out	**B** chilled out	**C** kept on
2	**A** turned down	**B** got into	**C** lived up to
3	**A** keep on	**B** split up	**C** chill out
4	**A** let down	**B** split up	**C** kept on
5	**A** keep on	**B** fall out	**C** turn down
6	**A** turn them down	**B** get into them	**C** let them down
7	**A** fell out	**B** turned it down	**C** split up with them
8	**A** let him down	**B** fall out with him	**C** live up to him

SPEAKING

Complete the conversations with the words in the box. There are two words you don't need.

crazy	enjoy	fan	into	mind
stand	bothered	thing		

1 **A:** We could watch a film on your phone.
   B: No. I can't _____ watching films on my phone – the screen's far too small!

2 **A:** Do you want to go bowling later?
   B: No, I don't like bowling – it isn't my _____.

3 **A:** Did you enjoy that film?
   B: Yes. I'm not usually a _____ of romantic films, but this one was quite good.

4 **A:** Does your sister like that new band, New Day?
   B: Yes, they're her favourite band now. She's completely _____ about them!

5 **A:** Have you heard the new song by Tamara?
   B: Yes, it's great. I'm really _____ her music.

6 **A:** Where do you want to sit?
   B: Well, I don't _____ sitting near the back of the cinema, but I'd prefer to be nearer the front.

WRITING

1 Complete the beginnings and endings for emails with the words in the box.

Bye	Dear	Hi (x2)	Looking	See	to seeing

Email beginnings:
1 _____,
2 _____ Anna,
3 _____ Anna,

Email endings:
4 _____ for now.
5 _____ you soon.
6 _____ forward _____ you.

2 We often use short forms in informal emails. Write one short form for each sentence.

1 There is a concert next Saturday. _____*There's*_____
2 Where is the festival taking place? _____
3 I will get the tickets. _____
4 I would love to come with you. _____
5 That is a really nice idea. _____
6 Jack is coming to the concert with us. _____

3 Choose the correct words in the messages.

Hi Lucas,
[1]*Would / Do* you like to come for a pizza with me tonight? We [2]*could / may* meet in town, if you like.
Hope you can come!
Sam

Hi Sam,
Thanks for the invitation. [3]*Sorry, but / No, but* I have to revise tonight because I've got exams tomorrow. How about [4]*go / going* tomorrow night instead?
Bye for now,
Lucas

Hi Lucas,
[5]*That sounds / That's* a nice idea. Let's [6]*meet / meeting* at seven o'clock. Why [7]*we don't / don't we* ask Kallum to come too?
Looking forward to seeing you,
Sam

4 Look at the sentences in exercise 3. Are they suggestions, invitations or responses? Write S, I or R.

1 _____   3 _____   5 _____   7 _____
2 _____   4 _____   6 _____

3 DINING OUT, EATING IN

VOCABULARY

1 Unjumble the letters in brackets to complete what Laura says about a meal. Then use the shaded letters to answer the question below.

I had a **1** _____ (lema) in an Italian restaurant last night, with some friends. I had a **2** _____ (lowb) of really nice soup first, as a **3** _____ (artster). I couldn't decide which **4** _____ (hisd) to have for my main **5** _____ (croseu). In the end I had fish. It was nice, but there was too much food on my **6** _____ (lapet) and I couldn't finish it all. I did manage some ice cream for dessert, though! When the **7** _____ (lilb) came, I was surprised because it wasn't too expensive. We left a big **8** _____ (pti) for the waiter, because he was really helpful.

Which part of the meal did Laura enjoy the most?
d _____

2 Choose the correct words to complete the comments about a new restaurant.

You should definitely try this restaurant. It **1** ___ really good food!

Excellent food, but quite busy, so you need to **2** ___ a table before you go.

We don't often **3** ___ out for dinner, but we thought we'd try it. We weren't disappointed!

The waiter was really friendly when he **4** ___ us to our table.

It was a bit slow. We waited quite a long time for the waiter to **5** ___ us the menu.

Very helpful waitress. She **6** ___ our coats and helped us choose what to eat.

We **7** ___ our food at 7.30 and didn't eat until 8.30!

Very expensive. When I **8** ___ for the bill, I couldn't believe how much it was!!

1	**A** gives	**B** serves	**C** brings
2	**A** choose	**B** keep	**C** reserve
3	**A** go	**B** take	**C** spend
4	**A** asked	**B** showed	**C** put
5	**A** take	**B** carry	**C** bring
6	**A** lifted	**B** removed	**C** took
7	**A** ordered	**B** asked	**C** demanded
8	**A** invited	**B** offered	**C** asked

3 Choose the correct words to complete the recipe.

Pasta with mushroom sauce

Chop some onions and garlic into small pieces, and slice the mushrooms. **1**Fry / Grate / Grill these for a few minutes in a large pan, in a small amount of oil. **2**Pour / Add / Mix salt and pepper and some fresh herbs, and a little cream. **3**Grate / Mix / Grill everything together in the pan, and **4**add / heat / slice gently for a few minutes. Meanwhile, boil some pasta in water. To serve, **5**mix / put / slice the pasta onto the plate and **6**heat / pour / mix the mushroom sauce over the pasta. **7**Fry / Grate / Heat a little cheese over the top. Delicious!

GRAMMAR

1 Choose the correct modifier in the sentences.

1 Mmm, this soup tastes *very / absolutely* delicious!
2 Those biscuits look *quite / absolutely* nice.
3 That fish smells *really / absolutely* good.
4 Those desserts look *extremely / absolutely* gorgeous!
5 Ooh, this ice cream is *extremely / absolutely* tasty!
6 I'm sorry, but that smells *very / really* disgusting!

2 Choose the correct word to complete the sentences.

1 Shall I add a _____ salt to the soup? (few / little)
2 There isn't _____ ice cream in the freezer. (any / no)
3 There are a _____ biscuits left. Would you like one? (few / little)
4 There isn't _____ milk in the fridge. (many / much)
5 There are _____ onions in this recipe. (any / no)

3 Complete the conversations with words from the box. There is one word you don't need.

a	an	any	few	little
lot	many	much	some	

A: How **1** _____ apples do we need for this recipe?
B: We only need a **2** _____ – just two or three, I think.

A: Would you like **3** _____ coffee?
B: No thanks. I don't drink **4** _____ coffee – just one cup in the morning.

A: I'm thirsty. Is there **5** _____ apple juice in the fridge?
B: No, but there's a **6** _____ orange juice. Would you like that?

A: We've got a **7** _____ of eggs in the fridge. Shall I make **8** _____ omelette for lunch?
B: Yes, that would be lovely!

4 Complete the second sentence so it has the same meaning as the first.

1 We don't have many eggs.
We only have _____ eggs.

2 There's no cake left!
There isn't _____ cake left!

3 I don't usually add much salt when I'm cooking.
I don't usually add a _____ of salt when I'm cooking.

4 There isn't much coffee in the jar.
There's only _____ coffee in the jar.

5 I don't have a lot of recipe books.
I only have _____ recipe books.

5 Complete the sentences with *a*, *an*, *the* or Ø (zero article).

1 Do you like _____ strawberries?

2 I need _____ glass of water.

3 Where's _____ cake that I bought yesterday?

4 Would you like _____ orange?

5 I don't usually have _____ sugar in my coffee.

6 Can you put _____ milk back in the fridge, please?

7 She's a vegetarian, so she doesn't eat _____ meat.

8 Would you like _____ slice of bread?

6 Choose the correct words to complete the blog post.

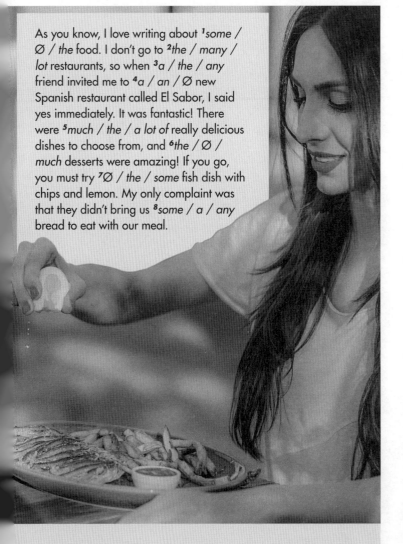

As you know, I love writing about ¹*some /
Ø / the* food. I don't go to ²*the / many /
lot* restaurants, so when ³*a / the / any*
friend invited me to ⁴*a / an / Ø* new
Spanish restaurant called El Sabor, I said
yes immediately. It was fantastic! There
were ⁵*much / the / a lot* of really delicious
dishes to choose from, and ⁶*the / Ø /
much* desserts were amazing! If you go,
you must try ⁷*Ø / the / some* fish dish with
chips and lemon. My only complaint was
that they didn't bring us ⁸*some / a / any*
bread to eat with our meal.

LISTENING

1 🔊 06 **Listen to the first part of an interview with Elsa, a food journalist, about a restaurant in New York. What is different about this restaurant?**

A All the cooks are grandmothers.

B The people who cook are all training to be chefs.

C You don't have to pay for the food.

2 🔊 07 **Listen to the rest of the interview and choose the correct answers.**

1 How did Elsa learn about this restaurant?
A A friend told her about it.
B She read a review of it online.
C She drove past an advertisement for it.

2 Mr Scaravella started the restaurant because
A he was fed up with eating in expensive restaurants.
B he wanted to remember his own grandmother's food.
C he wanted to encourage people to eat out more.

3 What do we learn about the menu?
A All the dishes are completely different every night.
B There are dishes from a different country every night.
C Some of the dishes are not very popular.

4 The different women who cook at the restaurant
A all compete with each other to make the best dishes.
B don't like tasting each other's food.
C give each other new ideas for cooking.

5 What do we learn about the cooking classes at the restaurant?
A You don't have to book in advance.
B They are free.
C They are only for women.

6 What did Elsa most enjoy about the experience?
A the food
B the atmosphere
C talking to other guests

Five sentences have been removed from the text below.

For each question, choose the correct answer.

There are three extra sentences which you do not need to use.

SWEETS – an ancient product

In a cave near Valencia in Spain there are paintings of people climbing trees to collect and eat the honey from bees' nests. Experts have studied these and reached the conclusion that they are eight thousand years old. **(1)** .... And that's not hard to understand because, for most people today, eating sweets is a very enjoyable thing to do.

The next time that sweet foods appear in history is around four thousand years ago in India. We know this from ancient texts that were written at that time in the Sanskrit language. **(2)** .... Sadly though, no-one knows exactly what they tasted like. We also know that the ancient Egyptians, Greeks and Romans all loved sweets, which they made by rolling fruit or nuts in honey. However, we now know that sugar was available in ancient Rome. **(3)** .... For this reason, sugar wasn't used for making sweets but for adding to medicines.

In Europe in the Middle Ages (the 6th–16th centuries) the price of sugar meant that only very rich people could afford sweets. **(4)** .... They could earn lots of money from having their own shop or from working in the palaces of kings and queens. Sweets were made by hand using boiled sugar or an ingredient called marzipan. It was common at the time to create sculptures of animals, castles, trees and even people. Some of the sculptures were huge and were presented to guests at formal dinners.

The kinds of sweets we recognise today were first made in the nineteenth century. The development of factories meant that sweets could be made in very large quantities. **(5)** .... The kinds of things they were able to buy were boiled sweets, chewing gum, toffee and chocolate.

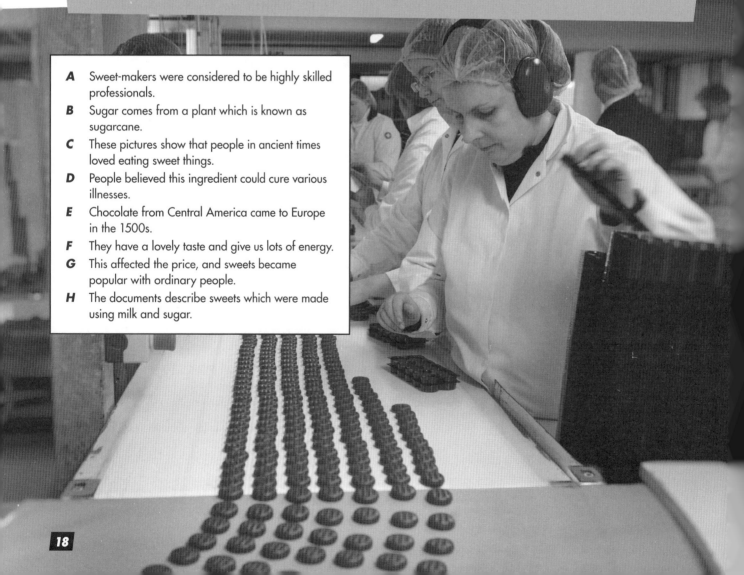

A Sweet-makers were considered to be highly skilled professionals.

B Sugar comes from a plant which is known as sugarcane.

C These pictures show that people in ancient times loved eating sweet things.

D People believed this ingredient could cure various illnesses.

E Chocolate from Central America came to Europe in the 1500s.

F They have a lovely taste and give us lots of energy.

G This affected the price, and sweets became popular with ordinary people.

H The documents describe sweets which were made using milk and sugar.

PUSH YOURSELF B2

1 Write the words in the correct order to make idioms.

1 piece / it's / cake / a / of

2 cup / not / of / tea / my / it's

3 pinch / take / salt / of / it / a / with / I'd

4 beans / he / the / spilt

5 all / pear-shaped / gone / it's

6 spilt / good / milk / no / it's / crying / over

2 Decide which idiom from exercise 1 could replace what each person said.

a It's happened and you can't change it now, so it's not worth worrying about it.

b It's really easy!

c Everything's gone wrong!

d He told them all about it!

e You definitely shouldn't believe that!

f I don't like that kind of thing.

2 Match the beginnings and ends of the sentences for talking about photographs.

1	This is a photo	a	are on the table.
2	There's	b	they're called.
3	I can	c	of a café.
4	I don't know what	d	for serving water.
5	People use them	e	like a large jug.
6	She's holding something. It looks	f	see four people.

WRITING

1 Complete the time expressions in the sentences with the correct words. There are three words you don't need.

after	at	end	finish	last
later	past	then	when	

1 I went out for a meal _____ weekend.

2 _____ the waiter arrived, she seemed very friendly.

3 _____ first, the food tasted a bit strange.

4 _____ a while, I started to enjoy it.

5 At the _____ of the meal, I felt very happy.

6 Our food arrived half an hour _____.

2 Choose the correct time expressions in the story.

I invited some friends to my flat for a meal ¹after a while / last Saturday. I like cooking, so I was happy to cook a meal for everyone. ²When they arrived / Next, we sat down at the table and I brought the food out. We started eating, but ³at first / then everyone started coughing. There was too much pepper in the food! I brought some water, but it was no good. ⁴After a while / At the end of the meal, we decided that we really couldn't eat it. I was a bit upset ⁵at first / next, but then I saw the funny side of it. ⁶Next / At first, we had to decide what to do! We decided to order some pizzas, and we had a great evening together. ⁷At the end of the evening / Then they left, everyone thanked me and went home. I'm sure we'll continue to laugh about it for a long time!

SPEAKING

1 Look at the photo and choose the correct words to complete the text.

I can see a family. I'm ¹not sure / not being sure, but I think they're in a café, because there are spoons and forks on the table ²behind / in front of the glasses. There's a boy ³in / on the left. He ⁴holds / is holding something. I don't know what it is. It looks ⁵as / like a menu, or maybe a book. I think it's summer ⁶so / because they're wearing summer clothes, and the man ⁷at / in the back of the photo is wearing a sun hat.

4 CITY LIVING?

VOCABULARY

1 Write the words next to the definitions. There are two words you don't need.

> apartment block   nature   neighbourhood
> scenery   skyscraper   stream   valley   waterfall

1 a small river ....
2 the area where you live ....
3 a large building with lots of flats in it

....
4 water that falls from high up ....
5 a very tall building ....
6 an area of low land between two mountains

....

2 Complete the words in the sentences.

1 It was easy to get around the city because there were lots of s........np........ts showing us where things were.
2 The quickest way to travel across New York is to use the s........y.
3 Let's buy a burger from the f........t........k over there.
4 The city has an amazing sk........ne, with lots of tall buildings.
5 I love spending time outdoors with n........e all around me.
6 When we got to the top of the hill we stopped to enjoy the beautiful sc........y around us.

3 Read what the people say about the places. Match the adjectives with what the people say.

1 A lot of great and interesting things happen here! ....
2 It's always quiet here. ....
3 The people are very kind here. ....
4 Nothing ever happens here! ....
5 This place looks really lovely. ....
6 It's never quiet here! ....

a beautiful   c exciting   e friendly
b noisy   d peaceful   f boring

GRAMMAR

1 Complete the text with the past simple or past continuous form of the verbs.

It ¹........ (rain) when I
²........ (arrive) at Jo's apartment block,
so I quickly ³........ (run) up to the first floor
and ⁴........ (ring) the doorbell. While I
⁵........ (wait) for Jo to open the door,
I ⁶........ (check) my phone. Yes, it was the
right day and time for the party. I was surprised when there
was no answer. While I ⁷........ (think)
about what to do, I ⁸........ (see) another
friend arriving. 'Hi,' I said. 'Jo's not in.' 'But you're at the
wrong flat,' he said. 'Jo lives on the second floor.'

2 Join the sentences using *when* or *while*.

1 I was having a shower. The taxi arrived.
The taxi ....
....
2 Tom was waiting for the bus. He saw Sam.
Tom ....
....
3 Lia was living in London. She met Paul.
Lia ....
....

3 Complete the sentences with the past perfect form of the verbs.

1 The film .... (already / start) when
we got to the cinema.
2 Max .... (just / leave) the house
when I called.
3 I was excited because I ....
(never / try) waterskiing before.
4 .... (you / ever / visit)
the United States before you went to study there?

4 Complete the text with the past simple or past perfect form of the verbs.

I ¹........ (go) to Rome last summer.
I ²........ (never visit) Italy before,
so I was really excited, and I wasn't disappointed! The
ancient buildings ³........ (look) amazing!
I ⁴........ (find) it hard to believe that people
⁵........ (build) them so long ago, without
any modern machines! We ⁶........ (have)
some great pizzas, and I was really pleased because I
⁷........ (learn) a few phrases in Italian before
I went, and I ⁸........ (manage) to use them
while I was there.

1 Read the article about green skyscrapers. What does the article discuss? Choose the best answer.

A the reasons why green skyscrapers are still not very popular

B the advantages and disadvantages of green skyscrapers

C the experiences of people who live in green skyscrapers

The country in the city?

Cities are often noisy and dirty places, and many people prefer the peaceful atmosphere of the countryside, with open fields and forests. However, there are many good reasons to live in cities – jobs, exciting things to do and plenty of new people to meet. Some architects are now trying to bring the country into the city by creating 'green skyscrapers'.

The Bosco Verticale in Milan is a skyscraper which tries to create a 'forest in the sky'. It opened in 2014 and has two towers, one just over 100 metres high and the other around 80 metres high. Inside, it is mainly apartments, but there are also some offices. The special thing about this skyscraper is that there are nearly 1,000 trees, and also hundreds of smaller plants, growing all over it.

Skyscrapers like this are more difficult and more expensive to build. There are problems with planting trees so high up – not all kinds of trees can live in the strong winds at this height. Also, someone has to look after the plants, to water them in hot weather and cut them back when they grow too big, so they don't spoil the view for the people who live there. This could be a lot of work for the people who

live there, but at Bosco Verticale, a special team of professional gardeners takes care of it.

But green skyscrapers also bring a lot of benefits. The trees and plants clean the air, keep the apartments cool in hot weather and reduce the amount of noise that people hear inside the building. More importantly, most people would agree that they are much more attractive to look at than the usual metal and glass. Some architects believe that over the next 20 years green buildings could change the skyline of our cities, to make them look more like forests.

I visited Singapore recently, and stayed in the Parkroyal on Pickering hotel. This 'hotel in a garden' is a great example of a green skyscraper. The building is covered in plants, and there is a 'skygarden', where guests can sit and enjoy views of the city. There are plants everywhere, and I was amazed that there are even indoor waterfalls! Rooms aren't cheap, but the price is worth paying to get the chance to escape from the noise and dirt outside and enjoy a little bit of the countryside in the heart of the city.

2 Read the article again. Choose the correct answers.

1 In the first paragraph, what does the writer say about cities?

  A Most people find cities too noisy and dirty.

  B There are a lot of benefits to living in cities.

  C There are too many new buildings in cities.

2 What do we learn about Bosco Verticale?

  A There are more than two towers.

  B There are only apartments inside.

  C It has trees and other plants growing on it.

3 Why are some trees not suitable to use in green skyscrapers?

  A They don't like the weather conditions.

  B They are too expensive.

  C They need too much water in hot weather.

4 What do we learn about the plants at Bosco Verticale?

  A They often cause problems when they get too big.

  B People are paid to look after them.

  C The people who live there find it difficult to look after them.

5 According to the writer, what is the biggest advantage of green skyscrapers?

  A They keep the apartments cool.

  B They reduce pollution.

  C They look nicer than other buildings.

6 How did the writer feel about staying in the Parkroyal on Pickering hotel?

  A disappointed at the views from the skygarden

  B surprised that there are waterfalls inside the hotel

  C angry about the high prices

08 For each question, choose the correct answer.

1 Where will the woman go camping this summer?

A   B   C

2 What's the view from the apartment block?

A   B   C

3 Which activity did the woman help with?

A   B   C

4 Where will the friends meet before going to the theatre?

A   B   C

5 Where is the problem in the apartment building?

A   B   C

6 What did the woman do in the park?

A   B   C

7 Where in the city will they eat tonight?

A   B   C

Choose the correct verb forms to complete the text.

Last summer, my aunt and uncle **¹took / were taking / had taken** me for a walk in the countryside while I **²stayed / was staying / had stayed** with them. It was terrible! First, my feet **³got / were getting / had got** wet because I **⁴didn't bring / wasn't bringing / hadn't brought** any strong shoes with me. Then some cows **⁵ran / were running / had run** after us while we **⁶walked / were walking / had walked** through a field. Finally, we **⁷spent / were spending / had spent** hours trying to find our way back because my uncle **⁸forgot / was forgetting / had forgotten** to bring the map with him. I think I'll stay in the city this year!

SPEAKING

1 Complete the conversations with the words in the box.

about	better	could	idea	let's
like	shall	sounds	sure	that's

A: What do you want to do today?

B: What **¹**_____ going to the park? There's a concert there this afternoon.

A: That **²**_____ good.

A: **³**_____ we go to the beach this afternoon?

B: I'm not **⁴**_____. It isn't very warm!

A: It's a lovely evening. We **⁵**_____ have a barbecue!

B: That's a nice **⁶**_____. I'll invite some friends.

A: Yes, **⁷**_____ great!

A: **⁸**_____ go shopping today.

B: I don't really **⁹**_____ that idea. I don't like shopping. There's a good film on at the cinema, though.

A: Yes, OK. I think that's a **¹⁰**_____ idea.

2 Choose the correct response.

1 We could go for a pizza if you like.
  A Yes, I like.
  B That sounds good.
  C Shall we go?

2 What about watching a movie tonight?
  A That was great.
  B No, I don't want.
  C I think that's a great idea.

3 We could go ice skating.
  A I don't think that's a better idea.
  B Yes, what about it?
  C Hmm, I don't really like that idea.

4 Let's meet at 7.30.
  A That looks good.
  B Yes, that's great.
  C I don't really like 7.30.

5 Shall we organise a party?
  A I'm not sure.
  B That's good.
  C I love that!

6 What about buying Anna some earrings for her birthday?
  A Yes, let's buy.
  B No, we couldn't.
  C That's a nice idea.

WRITING

1 Complete the sentences with the words in the box. There is one word you don't need.

after	end	first	later	next	when	while

1 We walked round the shops all afternoon, and the _____ day, my feet really hurt!

2 We visited the art gallery and _____ that we went for a coffee.

3 I was really worried, but in the _____ everything was fine.

4 At _____ I thought Freddie was joking, but then I realised he was serious.

5 I saw Sara again _____, at the sports centre.

6 I was walking home _____ I suddenly noticed I didn't have my bag with me.

2 Choose the correct time linkers in the story.

It was my birthday on Saturday. **¹While / At first** I was getting dressed in the morning, the doorbell rang. I opened the door and saw a big group of my friends. 'We're taking you out,' they said. We went for a coffee first, and **²then / at first** we went to a big theme park near the town. We spent a few hours there, having a great time, and **³when / after that** we went back into town for something to eat. **⁴Later / When**, we all went back to one friend's flat and we watched a movie together. I was really tired but happy when I **⁵in the end / finally** got home. It was an amazing day.

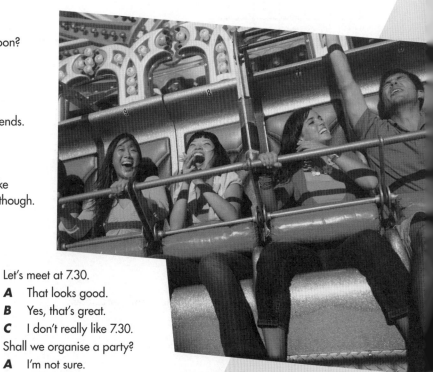

5 PICTURE OF HEALTH

VOCABULARY

1 Read the clues and complete the puzzle. Then use the shaded letters to complete the sentence.

1 It's all over your body.
2 You bend it if you want to jump.
3 The femur is the longest one in your body.
4 You use it when you breathe.
5 You move it when you wave your hand.
6 It joins your foot to your leg.
7 If you lift heavy things, it will get bigger and stronger.
8 You can't talk without it.
9 It's at the top of your arm.

1		K						
2			E					
3		O						
4				G				
5					T			
6			K					
7				C				
8			N					
9				L				

10 Anna fell and hurt her _____ _____ _____ _____ .

2 Complete what Marco says about his health.

I feel really ¹i _____ today. I think I've got a bad ²c _____ d. I've got a terrible ³s _____ e t _____ t, so I can't eat or drink anything, and I've also got a ⁴c _____ h, which gets worse every time I speak. I've got ⁵e _____ e in both my ears, and I can't walk around very much because I've got ⁶b _____ k _____ e! The only thing I can really do comfortably is lie on my bed and play computer games!

3 Choose the correct words to complete the sentences.

1 Be careful, or you'll *injury / injure / pain* yourself.
2 What happened to your arm? Is it *pain / pains / painful*?
3 Don't lift that heavy box – you might *sore / hurt / injury* your back.
4 My arm is really *pain / injury / sore* from falling off my bike.
5 I think you should go to the hospital – that looks like a serious *hurt / sore / injury*.

4 Complete the notice with the words in the box.

> emergency   infection   patients
> prescription   tablets

Important notice

If you have an appointment with the doctor, please wait in the waiting area. There may be other ¹ _____ before you, so please wait until your name is called. If the doctor gives you a ² _____ , you can collect your medicines at the chemist's on Broad Street. Children are usually given liquid medicines but if you would prefer ³ _____ for your child, please tell the doctor. If you are seriously ill and think the situation is an ⁴ _____ , please speak to the receptionist and she will call an ambulance. If you have an ⁵ _____ which might be dangerous to other people, please do NOT come to the clinic. Call us, and we will arrange for the doctor to visit you at home.

GRAMMAR

1 Complete the second sentence so it has a similar meaning to the first. Use the correct form of the word in brackets.

1 I wasn't able to dive when I was younger.
  I _____ when I was younger. (can)
2 I was able to ski when I was six!
  I _____ when I was six! (can)
3 My baby cousin can walk now!
  My baby cousin _____ now. (able)
4 I couldn't finish the race.
  I _____ the race. (able)
5 My grandma isn't able to run marathons any more.
  My grandma _____ marathons any more. (can)

2 Choose the correct words to complete the sentences.

1 You should *do / to do* more exercise.
2 I think you *ought to / ought* go to bed earlier.
3 You shouldn't *eating / eat* so much chocolate.
4 I don't think you *ought to / don't ought to* spend so much time playing on your computer.
5 You *shouldn't / don't ought to* drink so many sweet drinks.

3 Choose the correct words to complete the online posts.

Abi44G
I want to get fit quickly. I'm really unfit at the moment, and I ¹____ even run for a bus! I ²____ get to a gym because there isn't one near my house. Any ideas?

MaxPP
You ³____ start slowly and build up your fitness over a few months. Try walking to start with, and soon you ⁴____ run!

SamT99
You ⁵____ worry about not being near a gym. There's lots of gym equipment that you ⁶____ use at home, and it isn't expensive if you buy second-hand. Stop making excuses!

FitAmy
You definitely ⁷____ get a bike. I ⁸____ even ride a bike six months ago, but now I cycle everywhere, and it's a really great way to get fit!

1	**A** can't	**B** couldn't	**C** should
2	**A** ought to	**B** 'm not able to	**C** shouldn't
3	**A** couldn't	**B** ought	**C** should
4	**A** can	**B** were able to	**C** 'll be able to
5	**A** shouldn't	**B** could	**C** ought to
6	**A** can	**B** aren't able to	**C** shouldn't
7	**A** ought to	**B** can't	**C** were able to
8	**A** can't	**B** weren't able to	**C** couldn't

4 Complete the gym rules with the correct verbs. There is one verb you don't need.

don't need to book	don't have to bring	have to ask
must have	mustn't book	mustn't use	need to know

GYM RULES

1 All members _____ their membership cards with them at all times.

2 You _____ classes in advance, but it is a good idea for popular classes.

3 Junior members under 14 _____ the pool without an adult.

4 All members _____ for permission from a member of staff before using the heaviest weights.

5 Please use a gym towel when exercising. You _____ your own – you can get one at the reception desk.

6 Remember, our staff _____ if you have a health problem. Please don't forget to tell us!

5 Choose the correct words to complete the tips on how to train for a marathon.

The first thing to do is stop delaying and start training! If you ¹*couldn't / can't / aren't able* to run very far when you start, don't worry – everyone ²*could / has to / ought* start somewhere, and you'll soon get fitter. You ³*must / could / need* have a training programme – that's really important. The main idea of your programme is to slowly increase the distance you ⁴*could / are able / can* comfortably run, until a marathon doesn't seem such a scary idea. You ⁵*have to / ought / don't need to* run every day, but you ⁶*ought / should / are able to* try to run at least three times a week. In the last two weeks before the marathon, you ⁷*need / ought to / shouldn't* do less, not more. This sounds crazy, but you really ⁸*mustn't / don't have to / ought to* get an injury just before the big race – after all your hard work, you want to make sure you enjoy your big day!

PUSH YOURSELF B2

Match the beginnings and ends of the sentences.

1 I've got a splitting ____
2 Lots of people are ill at the moment. I think there's a ____
3 I was in bed all last week, but now I'm back ____
4 I don't feel well. I think I'm coming ____
5 Jill's been really ill, but luckily she's on the ____
6 I feel too ill to go to work today. I think I'll ____
7 I've walked 30 kilometres today, and now my ____
8 I feel really tired today. I think I'm a bit ____

a call in sick.
b mend now.
c bug going around.
d feet are killing me.
e on my feet.
f under the weather.
g headache. I need to take something for the pain.
h down with flu.

READING PART 6

For each question, write the correct answer.

Write one word for each gap.

To: Laura
Subject: Poor you!

Hi,

I'm really sorry to hear you broke your leg during the half-marathon on Saturday. You poor thing!

I was so surprised to get your email because you've **1** _____ had an accident while running before. As you say, at least **2** _____ were lots of people around you to help. And it was lucky you didn't have to wait **3** _____ long time for the ambulance to arrive to take you to hospital. Did the doctor say how long **4** _____ will be before you can run again?

Would you like me to **5** _____ some shopping for you, cook you a meal or take you to your hospital appointments? Just let me know if I can help **6** _____ all.

Janie

LISTENING

1 09 **Listen to a radio show about fitness apps. Which app does Jake suggest for Elly?**

A Ten-minute Yoga
B Daily Fit Club
C Burn the Fat
D Superfit in Ten

2 09 **Listen again. Decide if the sentences are true or false.**

1 Elly thinks she is already quite fit.
2 With *Ten-minute Yoga*, you do the same exercises each day.
3 Jake says it's difficult to read the instructions during the workouts with *Ten-minute Yoga*.
4 Jake says the trainer doesn't explain how to do the exercises on *Daily Fit Club*.
5 *Daily Fit Club* is good for people who haven't done much exercise before.
6 Jake says that the workouts on *Burn the Fat* seem very quick.
7 Jake thinks most people would find *Burn the Fat* boring.
8 The first workouts on *Superfit in Ten* are the most difficult.
9 Jake says Elly will only get fitter if she exercises regularly.

SPEAKING

1 Match the beginnings and ends of the phrases for asking about problems, showing sympathy and giving advice.

1	How are	**a**	care.
2	What's	**b**	having a nice hot drink?
3	Take	**c**	wrong?
4	Get	**d**	idea to put ice on an injury like that.
5	You ought	**e**	well soon.
6	Why don't you	**f**	go and see the doctor?
7	How about	**g**	you doing?
8	It's a good	**h**	to stay in bed today.

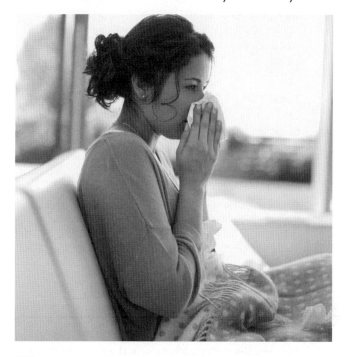

2 Complete the conversations with words from the box.

> feel better   how are   I were you   look after
> matter   poor   sorry to hear   why don't you

A: Hi, Amy, ¹_____ you?

B: Not very well. I think I've got flu.

A: Oh, I hope you ²_____ soon.

A: Hi, George. You look terrible! What's the ³_____?

B: I've got a really bad headache.

A: I'm ⁴_____ that. If ⁵_____, I'd go home and go to bed.

A: Oh, my leg's still really sore from the injury I got on Saturday.

B: ⁶_____ you! ⁷_____ go home and rest it?

A: I can't today. I have to go to work. But I'll rest tomorrow.

B: Well, ⁸_____ yourself!

A: Thanks, I will.

WRITING

1 Add one more letter to correct the spelling mistake in each sentence.

1 I hurt a musle in my leg. _____

2 I've got an apointment to see the doctor. _____

3 Your elbow is in the midle of your arm. _____

4 I've got backace! _____

5 You need your tonge to speak. _____

6 It hurts when I bend my nee. _____

7 I try to eat helthy food. _____

8 My lungs hurt when I breath in. _____

2 Read the email. Correct six mistakes with punctuation, four mistakes with prepositions and two mistakes with modal verbs.

> ● ● ● ◁ ▷   ⌕ 🏠
>   Reply Forward ✉
>
> Hi Jan
>
> Thanks to your email. You dont need to worry after me now – Im feeling much better. Youre definitely right that I should still to rest, though. I don't want to, but I know it's good to me.
>
> Dan's been brilliant. Hes really looked for me well! Ive got some new medicine now – I can't for remember its name, but its really good, so I hope I might be better soon.
>
> Emma

Punctuation:
_____
_____
_____
_____
_____
_____

Prepositions:
_____
_____
_____

Modal verbs:
_____
_____

6 ONLINE, OFFLINE

VOCABULARY

1 Read the clues and complete the crossword.

```
1        2     3  T
     4             5
6  O        O      D
                   
        7  E    E  T
     8     G
```

Across

2 When you … a photo or piece of writing, you put it online.

6 If you … someone, you see all the updates that they put on Instagram.

7 If you send someone a friend …, you ask them to be a friend online.

8 When you … someone, you add their name to a photo.

Down

1 If you … someone, you stop them seeing photos and things you write.

3 A … is a photo you take of yourself.

4 A … is something you write when a friend has put something online.

5 An … is when you give new information.

2 Choose the correct words to complete the sentences.

1 Carl was being really annoying online, so I *updated / unfriended* him.

2 Hana's just posted a new *story / filter* about her trip to Paris.

3 I don't change my online *status / selfie* very often.

4 Chloe loves using face *comments / filters* – they're really funny!

5 How often do you *update / request* your social media?

6 Ben is worried because he doesn't get many friend *comments / requests*.

3 Read the problem and comments. Complete them with the correct form of the verbs in the box.

break	get	grow	hit	make	rely	turn

LolaB

I'm feeling a bit sad because I **1**_____ up with my boyfriend last month. We gradually **2**_____ apart and in the end we had a big argument and I decided to end the relationship. I don't want to **3**_____ up with him, but I miss him and I can't imagine meeting anyone else. Any ideas?

TomG77

Why don't you **4**_____ to your friends for help? See if they can introduce you to someone new, and you never know – you might **5**_____ it off!

MiaKat

I don't agree with TomG. It isn't fair to **6**_____ on friends to find you a new boyfriend. Why not try a dating app? There's definitely someone out there that you can **7**_____ on well with! Good luck!

GRAMMAR

1 Complete the conversations with the correct form of *will* or *going to* and the verbs in brackets. Think about whether each verb is about a plan, or a decision that someone makes at the time of speaking.

A: Congratulations on your new job in London. When **1**_____ (you / move) there?

B: I'm not sure. I need to find a flat first.

A: Oh, I **2**_____ (help) you look! I love looking at flats!

A: **3**_____ (Harry / come) for a meal with us next weekend?

B: I don't know. I haven't seen him for ages. Maybe I **4**_____ (text) him later to invite him.

A: What's that?

B: It's a book about apps. I **5**_____ (do) a course next year on how to develop new apps.

A: That sounds interesting.

B: I **6**_____ (lend) you the book if you like.

A: Cool.

2 Choose the correct verb forms. Think about whether each verb is about an arrangement or a 'timetable future'.

1 Don't forget we *go / 're going* to the cinema this evening. The film *starts / 's starting* at seven, so don't be late!

2 What *do you do / are you doing* tomorrow evening? Do you want to meet for something to eat?

3 Where are you? You should be here at the station with me. The train *leaves / 's leaving* in 10 minutes!

4 Sorry, I can't come to football training with you this evening. I *meet / 'm meeting* Emma for a drink.

5 Can't chat now. I need to get some food and the supermarket *closes / 's closing* at six.

6 *Do you see / Are you seeing* Paul tomorrow? If so, can you remind him he owes me some money?

3 Complete the predictions with the correct form of *will* or *going to* and the verbs in brackets. Think about whether each one is a general prediction or a prediction where there is a sign that something is going to happen.

1 Oh, no! It's 8.30 already. I _____ (miss) my train!

2 I think travel _____ (be) more expensive in the future, so people _____ (not travel) so much.

3 Look at the sky! I think it _____ (rain).

4 We _____ (not need) to take a driving test in the future because our cars _____ (drive) themselves!

5 Do you think that people _____ (ever / live) on Mars?

6 Sam works really hard, so it's obvious that he _____ (pass) all his exams.

4 Choose the correct verbs to complete the student's thoughts.

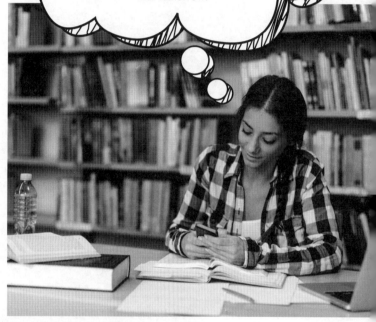

So, college ¹*starts / will start* again today. This year is my final year, so I know it ²*is / 's going to be* difficult. I want to do well, so I ³*'ll work / 'm going to work* really hard, especially at English. I ⁴*'ll meet / 'm meeting* my English teacher this afternoon to talk about things I can do at home to help me improve. I'm sure she ⁵*'ll have / 's having* some good ideas. As part of my plan, I ⁶*'ll stop / 'm going to stop* using social media so much – at the moment I check my phone every few minutes and it really stops me from studying! So I ⁷*don't check / 'm not going to check* my phone until I get home in the evening. But I've just had a message, so I ⁸*'ll start / 'm going to start* that tomorrow!

LISTENING PART 3

🔊 10 For each question, write the correct answer in the gap.

Write one or two words or a number or a date or a time.

You will hear a journalist called Steffi talking about a week she spent without using social media.

Steffi's Week without Social Media
Steffi started using social media at (**1**) _____.
Steffi mainly used social media for posting (**2**) _____.
Steffi realised she was spending at least (**3**) _____ every day on social media.
When she gave up using social media, Steffi read a (**4**) _____ instead.
After one week without social media, Steffi felt less (**5**) _____.
Steffi plans to use a (**6**) _____ app once a day.

READING

1 Read the article about the future of social media. Choose the best heading for each section A–D. There is one heading you don't need.

1 Bringing the world closer together
2 New ways to use your smartphone
3 The end of the screen
4 New ways to hang out with friends
5 Connected to everything and everyone

What's the future of social media?

Read the opinions of four experts

Twenty-five years ago there was no social media – no Facebook or Instagram, no tweets or sharing of photos. Social media has changed our lives a lot, but where will it be in twenty years' time? We asked four experts.

PUSH YOURSELF **B2**

Complete the second sentence so it has a similar meaning to the first. Use the word in brackets.

1 I'm fairly sure that people will travel to Mars one day.
People _____
to Mars one day. (probably)

2 It isn't likely that machines will do all the work for us.
I _____
do all the work for us. (doubt)

3 It's likely that computers will become even smaller.
There's a _____
become even smaller. (chance)

4 I'm sure people won't stop using their phones.
People _____
using their phones. (certainly)

5 It isn't likely that cities will become smaller.
There's _____
cities will become smaller. (chance)

6 I'm 100% certain that people will eat less meat in the future.
People _____
less meat in the future. (definitely)

A _____
All types of technology will use voice controls, so there won't be any more keyboards on our phones. Screens won't be important either, so wanting the latest smartphones with bigger and better screens will be a thing of the past. Instead, we will see holograms – images in the real world, in front of us, and they will look amazingly real. At the moment, we chat with a friend and we look at their face on our phone or computer. In 20 years, we'll be able to see them sitting next to us, looking very much like a real person.
Jacob Stone, Media Director

B _____
I think we will definitely have an electronic device inside our body which will connect us to everything around us. We will be connected to the machines in our homes and places of work, like our cookers and printers. We'll be connected to the internet too, so we'll be able to find information just by thinking about it. And, of course, we'll be connected to each other. I know it sounds a bit crazy at the moment, but I really believe it will be possible to share our thoughts and feelings with each other directly, even when we're in different parts of the world.
Alyssa Tyrone, Creative Manager

C _____
When events happen anywhere in the world, we won't need to send journalists to report on them. There will be hundreds of films, stories and messages from normal people who are there, showing the world what's happening, as it actually happens. People will also be able to share smells and tastes, and even feelings, so it will be possible for everyone to really experience what is happening in another part of the world, whether it's a terrible flood or a fire, a big sporting event or a cultural celebration. We will all feel more connected to each other, and the world will feel a much smaller place.
Amelia Smid, Digital News Editor

D _____
At the moment, I connect with my friends on social media by liking posts, writing comments and uploading photos. In 20 years, I'll disconnect from all this. I'll put on my special glasses and meet my friends in virtual worlds. It will be possible to choose the place, from a beach in Spain to a café in London, and I'll bring together people from my real life and my online friends to have social time together. We'll chat and share jokes, and the experience will feel completely real, even though we'll really all be in different places.
Dev Khan, Digital Product Developer

2 Read the predictions again. Which expert (A–D) thinks ...

1 we won't need a computer or phone to search for something online? _____
2 we won't care so much about the kind of phone we have? _____
3 we will be able to share experiences from all our senses? _____
4 ordinary people will report the news for us? _____
5 we will decide where in the world to see our friends? _____
6 talking to someone on the phone will feel more realistic? _____
7 our real friends and social media friends will meet each other? _____
8 some of the predictions seem difficult to believe right now? _____

SPEAKING

1 Choose the sentence that is NOT relevant as part of an answer to each question.

1 Where do you live?
- **A** I live in Berlin.
- **B** I'd like to visit Paris one day.
- **C** I enjoy living in a big city.

2 What do you do?
- **A** A lot of people want to work for a bank.
- **B** It's an interesting job.
- **C** I work for a bank.

3 How do you get to work or school every day?
- **A** I sometimes walk if the weather's fine.
- **B** 300 people work in my office.
- **C** The buses are usually very busy.

4 Do you think English will be useful for you in the future? Why? / Why not?
- **A** You need English for a lot of different jobs.
- **B** I'd like a job where I can travel a lot.
- **C** I'd like to learn some other languages in the future.

5 What does your family do together?
- **A** We sometimes go out for meals.
- **B** Some of my friends don't get on well with their families.
- **C** I enjoy spending time with my family.

6 Tell us about a teacher that you like.
- **A** I'm going to leave university next year.
- **B** His name is Mr Grigson.
- **C** I always enjoy the lessons.

2 Complete the phrases for gaining time.

1 What do you like doing in your free time?
Oh, lots of things. _____ _____ see … I really enjoy doing sport, and …

2 Tell us about the place where you live.
Hmm, _____ _____ where I live. It's a small town in the north of Italy …

3 How much time do you spend on social media?
_____, to be honest, I don't spend very much time on social media. I …

4 What do you like about your job or school?
Hmm, _____ _____ _____ about my job. I guess I meet a lot of people and I enjoy that because …

5 Where do you meet your friends?
OK, _____, I have a lot of friends and we often meet …

6 What do you find difficult about learning English?
Hmm, _____ _____ difficult. I think probably the most difficult thing for me is …

WRITING

1 Choose the correct words to complete the tips for writing a blog post.

1 It's a *good / bad* idea to show your own personality in what you write.

2 You should *use your own style / copy a successful style*.

3 Try to write *long / short* paragraphs so it doesn't get boring.

4 Use *a formal / an informal* tone.

5 *Ask questions / Make general statements* to help the reader feel involved.

6 *Invite / Don't invite* comments from your readers.

2 Read the sentences from a blog post about friends. Match each sentence that uses a formal tone (1–6) with one that uses an informal tone with a similar meaning (a–f).

1 Everyone understands the importance of friends in our lives. ....

2 There are times when you rely on a friend to give you support. ....

3 Sometimes you can recognise immediately that you will have a long friendship with someone. ....

4 Friends share both good and bad experiences with you. ....

5 Some of your friends may find it difficult to have good relationships with each other. ....

6 When you are experiencing problems, it is clear which of your friends are true friends. ....

a Sometimes you just know that someone will be a friend for life.

b It's hard to imagine life without friends, isn't it?

c When things go wrong, you can see who your real friends are.

d Friends are there for you in good times and bad.

e Sometimes you really need a friend to help you.

f Some of your friends may not hit it off with each other.

3 Choose the two openings that would make you keep reading a blog post about social media.

a Let me start by telling you one of my funniest social media stories.

b Social media is a complete waste of time. I never use social media, but prefer to spend real time with my friends and family.

c This post will discuss the history of social media and its importance in the world today.

d Do you love the way you can connect with people on social media? I certainly do! So, what new forms of social media are coming soon, and how will we use them?

7 WHAT'S YOUR STYLE?

VOCABULARY

1 Complete the conversation with the words in the box.

> afford   fit   look   style   suit   try

A: Oh, look at that dress! I love that long ¹_____,
and the colour would really ²_____ you.
You ³_____ great in blue! Why don't you
⁴_____ it on?

B: It's lovely, but the only size they've got is small, and
I don't think that will ⁵_____ me. Anyway,
I can't ⁶_____ to buy any more clothes!

2 Complete the words in the online adverts.

> A ¹l_____s____ white shirt with blue
> ²st_____p____s and a white ³c_____r.
> There are a few ⁴b____t_____s missing, but
> otherwise it's in perfect condition.
>
> **£3.99** **BUY IT NOW!**

> Two dresses, both with long ⁵s_____v____s,
> one ⁶p_____n red, the other blue with a
> flowery ⁷p__t_____n. Only worn once,
> but now too ⁸t____g____t for me.
>
> **£10 each** **BUY IT NOW!**

3 Read the clues and complete the puzzle. Then
complete the sentence with the shaded word.

(crossword grid with letters: O, S, P, G, T, D, Y, N, Y)

1 not neat or tidy
2 an arrangement of things for sale in a shop
3 things that are sold in a shop
4 something that seems cheaper than it should be

This shop likes to keep its _____ happy!

4 Complete the shop review with the correct words.
There are two words you don't need.

> messy   offers   products   reduced
> reductions   sales   shoppers   value

Most ¹_____ will love this shop! Some of the
displays in the shop window look a bit ²_____,
but don't let that put you off. The ³_____ that
they sell are all great, and really good ⁴_____
for money. There are often some great price
⁵_____, and they regularly have special
⁶_____ like two for the price of one.
Definitely worth a visit!

5 Choose the correct words to complete the email.

Dear customer,

Thank you for your recent ¹*order / refund* from
our website for ²*a / some* Superfit jeans and
three other items. Your ³*return / receipt* is
attached to this email. Your goods will be
⁴*ordered / delivered* to your home address
within three days. If the goods are ⁵*damaged /
exchanged* in any way, please ⁶*exchange /
return* them to us immediately and we will
arrange for a full ⁷*receipt / refund* to be paid
into your account. If you wish to ⁸*deliver /
exchange* the goods for any other reason, please
send them back to us with a note explaining
what you would like to do.

GRAMMAR

1 Choose the correct verb forms to complete the
reported speech.

1 'I bought my dress online.'
She said that she *bought / had bought / has bought*
her dress online.

2 'I never wear jeans to work!'
He said that he never *wore / had worn / has worn*
jeans to work.

3 'I can't afford to buy a lot of clothes.'
She said that she *can't afford / couldn't afford / won't
afford* to buy a lot of clothes.

4 'I've seen some great bargains in the sales.'
He said that he *saw / 's seen / had seen* some great
bargains in the sales.

2 Complete the reported speech. Remember to change the pronouns as well as the verb tenses.

> We've spent all our money!

1 My friends said that _____ money.

> I'd never been to that shop before.

2 Anna said that _____ that shop before.

> I can help you choose some new trainers.

3 I said to Dan that _____ some new trainers.

> I'll lend you my jacket.

4 I told Maria that _____ jacket.

> I love your new shirt.

5 Mia told me that _____ new shirt.

> I must get some new trainers!

6 Paul said that _____ new trainers.

3 Choose *say* or *tell*.

1 Al *said / told* me that he doesn't wear ties.
2 Carl *said / told* that the department store had some great bargains.
3 She didn't want to *say / tell* me how much she had paid for her boots.
4 The shop assistant *said / told* to me that this style was very popular.
5 Charlie *said / told* me all about her trip to London.
6 I asked her if the prices would be reduced, but she *said / told* no.

4 Read the questions and answers. Then complete the reported speech.

1
Paul: Where are you going?
Me: I'm going to the department store.
Paul asked me _____ .
I told _____
to the department store.

2
Anna: Do you like my new dress?
Me: It looks amazing!
Anna asked me _____
new dress.
I said _____ amazing.

3
Maria: When will you start your new job?
John: I'm not sure.
Maria asked John _____
new job.
John said _____ sure.

4
My sister: Did you find any bargains?
Me: I found a few.
My sister asked me _____
any bargains.
I told _____ a few.

5
Eva: What have you bought?
Me: I've bought some new shoes.
Eva asked me _____ .
I said _____ some new shoes.

6
Carlo: Are you going to ask for a refund?
Lisa: I've already done it.
Carlo asked Lisa _____
a refund.
Lisa said _____ it.

LISTENING

1 11 Listen to the first part of a podcast about clothes. What are *ethical* clothes?

A expensive clothes that are fashionable and look good
B clothes that are made in a way that doesn't harm the environment or people
C clothes that are cheap, so people can afford them

2 12 Listen to the rest of the podcast. Choose the sentence that sums up the ideas.

A Ethical clothes are good for the planet and people, and they also look good.
B Ethical clothes help animals and they are often cheaper than other clothes.
C Ethical clothes sound like a good idea, but they don't really exist.

3 12 Listen again. Answer the questions.

1 What is unusual about the trainers Kiera talks about?
2 What does this company no longer use in its stores?
3 What happens to most clothes when they go into the ground as rubbish?
4 What is different about the Swedish company's clothes?
5 What can people do if they can't afford to buy the Swedish company's clothes?
6 Why are some clothes on GoodClothes.com suitable for vegetarians?
7 Why does Kiera think she won't buy a T-shirt from GoodClothes.com?

Read the conversation between Milly and a shop assistant, then complete what Milly says about the conversation. For each sentence, choose one of the verbs in brackets.

Milly: OK. I'll take this bag, please.

Assistant: Lovely. Can you come to the till, please?

Milly: Of course. Is it possible to clean the bag if it gets dirty?

Assistant: Yes. If you need to clean it, you should use a special cleaner. We've got some here, for £6.00.

Milly: Right. I'll take that, too.

Assistant: OK. Now, it's important that you don't get this bag wet, otherwise the colour might come out.

Milly: OK. It's a present for a friend, Sara. Is it possible for her to exchange it, if she doesn't like it?

Assistant: Of course. Keep the receipt, and if she brings it back with the receipt we'll definitely exchange it for her.

Milly: Thanks.

Assistant: There you are. And would you like to come to our special sales evening? There will be some great price reductions.

Milly: Oh, yes please.

1 The shop assistant _____*asked me to come*_____ to the till. (warn / ask / promise)

2 She _____ a special cleaner on the bag. (invite / promise / advise)

3 She _____ the bag wet. (ask / warn / promise)

4 She _____ the bag if Sara doesn't like it. (invite / ask / promise)

5 She _____ the receipt. (tell / invite / warn)

6 She _____ come to a special sales evening. (promise / advise / invite)

For each question, choose the correct answer.

1
> These headphones can only be returned for a refund if the plastic box is unopened and in perfect condition.

A You won't be able to get your money back if you've damaged the box.

B If you don't like these headphones after using them, return them for a refund.

C These headphones are in the sale because the plastic box they're in is damaged.

2
> Wash at 30 degrees by hand or in machine, using any cleaning liquid suitable for silk. Always wash separately and dry flat.

A After washing this shirt by hand, hang it up to dry.

B Avoid washing this shirt together with other clothes.

C Any cleaning product may be used to wash this shirt.

3
> **Welcome to Unique Fashions** – the newest store on the web! Click here for a free gift in exchange for signing up to our weekly email.

A Unique Fashions are offering rewards to everyone placing their first web order.

B Customers who order online from Unique Fashions this week will receive a reward.

C There is a reward for anyone who agrees to receive emails from Unique Fashions.

4
> Daisy,
> I went to the 50% off sale at Greens Department Store. The jeans you bought were all gone but I got some fantastic bargains in the sports department, including a pair of trainers.
> Morgan

A Morgan found fewer bargains in the department store sale than Daisy did.

B Morgan bought something different to her friend Daisy in the sale.

C Morgan managed to buy some trainers at less than half the original price.

5
> ## Need a different size?
> Our changing room staff will be pleased to fetch this for you. Just ask.

A If you find something is too tight, changing room staff can bring a bigger size.

B Our changing room staff are happy to check for you what size you are.

C Please give anything that's the wrong size to changing room staff when you leave.

SPEAKING

1 Choose the correct words to complete the responses.

1 **A:** I'd love to go shopping in New York.
 B: So *would / do* I.

2 **A:** I often get new clothes for my birthday.
 B: *Also / Same* here.

3 **A:** I don't often buy things from department stores.
 B: Me *also / neither*.

4 **A:** I think it's much easier to shop online.
 B: I know what you *say / mean*.

5 **A:** I love it when the shops are really busy in the sales.
 B: *Would / Do* you? I hate it!

6 **A:** I always try shoes on before I buy them.
 B: I do *too / also*.

2 Choose the best response.

1 I don't like those trainers.
 A So do I.
 B Do you?
 C Neither do I.

2 I love bright colours!
 A That's a good point.
 B Same here.
 C So am I.

3 Sometimes it's difficult to find something that fits you.
 A Me too.
 B Do you?
 C I know what you mean.

4 I always get excited when the sales start.
 A So do I.
 B Me neither.
 C So am I.

5 A lot of clothes are cheaper online.
 A Me too.
 B That's a good point.
 C So do I.

6 I'd like to work for a fashion company.
 A Me neither.
 B I am too.
 C So would I.

WRITING

1 Match the beginnings and ends of these sentences for a review.

1 There's a very good selection ....
2 The best thing about ....
3 The only thing that's not good ....
4 It's definitely worth ....
5 I'd certainly ....
6 What I like ....
7 My only ....

a is the delivery time.
b recommend this site.
c of products.
d most about this site is how easy it is to use.
e this website is the prices.
f complaint is that the colours are too pale.
g checking out this site.

2 Decide if the sentences are positive or negative. Write P or N.

1 Their products are amazing quality. ....
2 The range is extremely limited. ....
3 Some of their things are not the best value. ....
4 There's an incredible variety of goods. ....
5 The prices are very reasonable. ....
6 They're rather expensive. ....

3 Choose the correct linking words.

1 *Although / But* the quality is good, the range is fairly limited.

2 The staff are extremely helpful *and / though* they certainly know all about the products.

3 There's a great variety of products. The prices are extremely high, *as well / though*.

4 The staff are really friendly, *but / and* they're often too busy to help you.

5 Most of their products are good quality, and the prices are very reasonable *as well / though*.

4 Complete the review with the words and phrases in the box. There are three you don't need.

as well	but	complaint	selection	like most
not so good	reasonable	recommend
the best thing	worth

This is an amazing online shoe shop! There's a great
¹ .... of shoes and boots, and the prices
are very ² .... What I ³ ....
about this website is the fact that they give extra
information like 'these shoes are best for people with
narrow feet.' My only ⁴ .... is that the shoes
took a week to arrive, ⁵ .... I'm really
pleased with them. It's definitely ⁶ ....
checking out this site, and I would certainly
⁷ .... their shoes!

VOCABULARY

1 Read the clues and complete the puzzle. Then put the shaded letters in order to answer the question.

¹C		V				
²	H	O				
³		V		S		
⁴C			F			
⁵S		N		S		
⁶	E		V		S	
⁷		V		B		K

1 It might be fun to explore inside here, but it's very dark.
2 I love walking along this, next to the sea.
3 If there's a storm at sea, these are very big.
4 I like climbing up this and then looking down at the sea below.
5 These can be big or small, and you find them on the ground.
6 All trees have these, and they're usually green.
7 You can sometimes walk along here, next to the river.
8 Where would Katy love to go? _____

2 Unjumble the letters to complete the sentences.

1 There were colourful birds on the _____ of the trees. (bnareshc)
2 It was fun walking across the _____ _____ in the desert. (dans dnesu)
3 You can't sail your boat over the _____! (werataﬂl)
4 There are no trees here, but there are lots of small _____. (shubes)
5 If you climb a high mountain, you may have to climb over a _____. (galcrie)
6 The ship sank when it hit an _____. (ciebreg)

3 Read what the people say about the places. Choose the correct adjective for each place.

1 There are no sounds here at all! — humid / quiet
2 There are so many bushes, we can't get through! — dense / dry
3 There's nothing in this cave! — noisy / empty
4 There's very little rain here. — dry / dense
5 There are so many birds here, and they're all singing! — quiet / noisy
6 It's hot here, and the air feels wet. — empty / humid

4 Complete the names of four habitats. Then match each one to a definition.

1 g_____ s_____ l_____ d s
2 t_____ p_____ l f_____ t s
3 t_____ m_____ r_____ e f_____ t s
4 p_____ l_____ r r_____ g_____ s

A It's very cold here for most of the year, and there's a lot of snow.
B There are very few trees or bushes here, but plenty of space for animals to move around.
C The trees and bushes are very dense, and it's also hot and humid.
D There are lots of trees here, and the weather is never too hot or too cold.

5 Read the clues and complete the animal names.

1 I'm a bird, but I can't fly. p_____ n
2 I've got big back legs and I move around by jumping. k_____ o
3 I'm small and brown, and I've got thin, sharp parts all over my body to protect me. h_____ g
4 I use my long neck to reach up and eat leaves on the trees. g_____ e
5 I'm a big, strong animal with thick, white fur and I live at the North Pole. p_____ r b_____ r
6 I'm small, I live in trees and I've got a thick tail. r_____ d s_____ l
7 I look like a big monkey, and I've got red fur. o_____ gu_____ n
8 I eat grass and live in large groups. I can run fast to escape from animals that hunt me. r_____ d d_____ r
9 I live in very cold areas, and you can often hear me calling at night. a_____ c w_____ f
10 I'm quite big and brightly coloured, and I've got hard skin, with no fur. g_____ n i_____ a

6 Complete the advert with the correct -ed or -ing adjectives based on the verbs.

RAINFOREST ADVENTURE!

Do you want a **¹**_____ (challenge) holiday this year? Why not come on a rainforest adventure! You definitely won't be **²**_____ (disappoint)! You'll see some **³**_____ (amaze) animals, and experience one of the most **⁴**_____ (excite) places on Earth! You don't need to feel **⁵**_____ (worry) about dangers, because the trip is carefully planned with safety in mind, and it ends with a **⁶**_____ (relax) few days in a luxury hotel. Visit our website today for more details – you'll be **⁷**_____ (surprise) how low our prices are!

GRAMMAR

1 Choose the correct modals of speculation to complete the email.

Hi Jo,

This is day five of my jungle adventure, and we're staying in a small hotel tonight – luxury! It's really hot, and there are dark clouds, so I think it **¹**could / must rain again soon. We can hear lots of monkeys in the jungle, but our guide says we **²**couldn't / may not see them because they stay high up in the trees. There are also lots of snakes, and I'm sure some of them **³**can / must be poisonous, which is a bit scary. We keep seeing things moving in the river. Freddie says they **⁴**can't / mustn't be crocodiles because there aren't any in this region, but I still think I **⁵**can / may stay well away from the water! It **⁶**can / might be a while before I can write again because we're going deeper into the jungle, and I'm sure there **⁷**can't / must be wi-fi there!

Take care,

Mia

2 Complete the second sentence so it has a similar meaning to the first. Choose the correct modal in brackets to give the correct meaning.

1 I'm sure Dan isn't scared of spiders!
Dan _____ of spiders!
(might / can't / must)

2 It's possible that I will go to Africa next summer.
I _____ to Africa next summer.
(may / can / must)

3 It's possible that we won't see any lions.
We _____ any lions.
(might not / couldn't / can't)

4 Maybe there are sharks in the water.
There _____ sharks in the water.
(can / could / must)

5 It's possible that there aren't any tigers here.
There _____ any tigers here.
(can't / may not / couldn't)

6 I'm sure it's difficult living in the Arctic Circle.
It _____ living in the Arctic Circle. (can / could / must)

PUSH YOURSELF **B2**

Complete the animal fact file with the correct words.

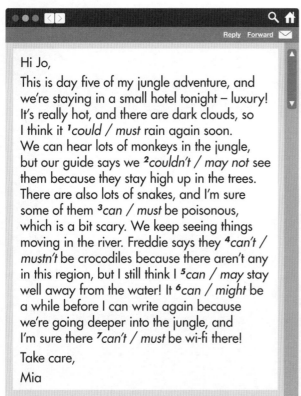

ANIMAL FACTS

1 Most kinds of deer have short t___i___s. The males use their a___t___rs for fighting.

2 Elephants can lift almost 350 kilos with their t___n___s. Unfortunately, they are often killed for their t___ks.

3 Some horses have long m___n___s which can grow down to their knees. Horses are not the only animals that have h___v___s – sheep, deer, camels and giraffes also have them.

4 Tigers' feet have soft p_____s but very sharp c_____ws, which can grow to over 10 cm long!

5 The Australian pelican is a large bird with black and white f_____th_____s. It has a very large b_____k which it uses for catching fish and which can be from 30 to 50 cm long!

READING

1 Read the article about wild swimming. Match the headings with the paragraphs. There is one heading you don't need.

1 Wild swimming in the city
2 What is wild swimming?
3 Bored with the swimming pool?
4 Why is it popular?
5 Is it safe?

2 Read the article again. Decide if the sentences are true or false.

1 Wild swimming is becoming more popular.
2 Wild swimmers accept that water in rivers and lakes isn't as clean as the water in swimming pools.
3 Most wild swimmers want to enjoy an extreme experience.
4 The main danger in rivers and lakes is from fast-moving water.
5 People can find safety advice about wild swimming online.
6 People have always swum in the canals in Paris.

A ....

There's nothing like the feeling of diving into cool water on a hot summer's day! But for some, the traditional swimming pool just isn't exciting enough. Instead, they are looking for something more challenging, and are turning to wild swimming in increasing numbers.

B ....

Wild swimming simply means swimming in a natural environment, like the sea, a river or a lake. Fans of the sport say that it is a great way to feel connected with the natural world. They also argue that, although pollution exists, natural water is generally cleaner than that in swimming pools because nothing is added to it, and it isn't full of crowds of people. For the few who are more adventurous, there is the extra challenge of finding more extreme places to test the water, like icy mountain lakes!

C ....

It must be exciting to swim in such places, but there are dangers, too, and anyone thinking of trying wild swimming should think carefully about safety. Many lakes and rivers are very deep. The water may be fast-moving, and it can be difficult to swim against this movement. But even more worrying than this, there could be hidden plants or rubbish under the surface. For this reason, it's a good idea to always walk into the water rather than diving in head first. To help people avoid the dangers, there are several websites which offer advice on safe places to swim.

D ....

But fortunately, it isn't only in the countryside that people can enjoy a wild swim. Many big cities have rivers and canals running through their centres, and some are now opening these to swimmers. In Paris, for example, people can now swim in one of the main canals in the city. Swimming wasn't allowed in the canal for nearly a hundred years because of pollution, but in 2017 the government declared that the water was safe and announced official swimming areas with safety officers to make sure there were no accidents. The swimmers soon took advantage of this in their thousands, as it perhaps offers the perfect solution of a wild swimming experience in a safe environment!

13 For each question, choose the correct answer.

You will hear an interview with a man called Rob Tucker, who is an expert on Australian camels.

1 Rob became interested in camels when he
   A read a book about a journey.
   B got a holiday job on a sheep farm.
   C saw a documentary film about camels.

2 Rob says that camels brought to Australia in the 1860s
   A were mainly from Arabian countries.
   B were stronger than camels born in Australia.
   C were accompanied by people who could ride them.

3 Why does Rob think camels were more useful than horses in Australia?
   A They could go for days without drinking water.
   B They could travel over difficult ground.
   C They could walk all day without needing breaks.

4 Why do some Australian farmers today complain about the camels?
   A They damage houses.
   B They break water pipes.
   C They eat the farm animals' food.

5 Rob recommends a camel ride that lasts
   A half a day.
   B one day.
   C three days.

6 Rob says it's sometimes hard to see camels in the wild because
   A they stay away from the roads.
   B their colour is similar to the landscape.
   C the camel population has recently decreased.

1 Choose the adjective which does NOT fit in each sentence.

1 There's a small restaurant near the beach which serves *fresh / relaxing / delicious* food.
2 You can walk along the *high / rocky / clear* cliffs.
3 It's lovely to swim in the lovely *long / cool / clear* water.
4 There are *amazing / high / fantastic* views from the top of the mountain.
5 There are also some very *fresh / interesting / exciting* towns to visit.
6 It's a great place to come for a *relaxing / rocky / long* holiday.

2 Choose the correct linking words.

1 Corsica is an island in the Mediterranean *and / but* it's a great place to visit.
2 *Although / But* it's quite small, there are lots of things to do.
3 Corsica is a part of France, *because / so* people speak French there.
4 There are plenty of beautiful beaches *as well as / also* mountains where you can go walking.
5 I love Corsica *because / so* it's so quiet and peaceful.
6 *What's more / Although*, there are lots of hotels which aren't too expensive.

Look at the photo and complete the sentences for describing it with the correct words.

background	can see	middle	might
must be	on	sure	there's	this is

1 .... a picture of a sports adventure.
2 .... a small beach, which is empty.
3 The sea is .... the right.
4 In the .... of the picture we .... a man.
5 He's running along the shore, and it .... quite cold because he's wearing long trousers and a sweatshirt.
6 There's a small object on the grass. I'm not .... what it is.
7 The man is carrying a rucksack. I guess it .... be to carry some food and drink.
8 In the .... , there are some tall cliffs.

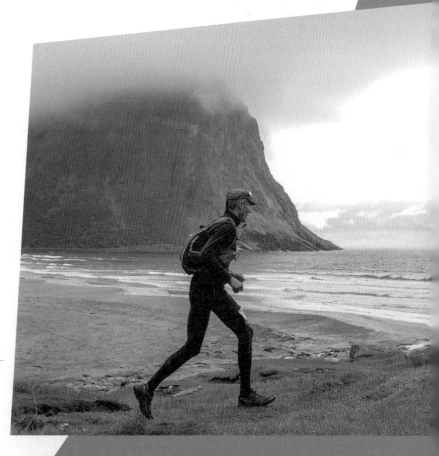

9 ALWAYS LEARNING

VOCABULARY

1 Complete what the student says about school. Use the highlighted letters to complete the final sentence.

> It's really important to ¹a _____ t _____ d school.
> ²E _____ c _____ _____ n is important, and it's difficult to get a good job if you don't have ³q ___ l _____ c _____ _____ s.
> I try to work hard for exams and I usually get good ⁴g _____ d _____ s. We also learn a lot of useful ⁵_ k _____ l _____ at school, like planning tasks and working together. The only thing I don't like about school is all the ⁶ _____ _____ !

2 Complete each sentence with two of the words given.

1 What's the _____ of tomorrow's _____? I hope it's interesting!
(degree / lecture / topic)

2 Did you _____ all your exams last _____? I hope you did!
(pass / term / tutor)

3 I can't believe that I'll _____ and get my _____ this summer!
(degree / fail / graduate)

4 It's simple – if you don't _____ enough, you'll _____ your exams!
(fail / revise / pass)

3 Choose the correct words to complete the tips.

HOW TO BE A TOP STUDENT

1 It's important to listen carefully in lectures. This will help you to *take / do* good notes.

2 Always *do / make* homework on time, so you're ready for the next piece of work.

3 *Pay / Give* attention when tutors or other people are talking to you.

4 Try to *do / make* extra research on your own, outside class.

5 If you *do / make* a mistake, learn from it!

6 Make sure you get enough sleep before you *make / take* an exam.

7 Be proud of yourself when you finally *get / make* your degree – it's a great achievement!

GRAMMAR

1 Choose the correct words to complete the passive sentences.

1 All students *is / are* expected to work hard.

2 Our maths class *is / was* cancelled yesterday.

3 We *was / were* told our exam results yesterday.

4 Lunch *is / are* served between 12.30 and 1.30.

5 I think that students now *are / were* given too much homework.

6 Spanish *doesn't / isn't* taught in all schools in the UK.

2 Complete the passive sentences.

1 Paul and Mel's parents sent them to a private school.
Paul and Mel _____ to a private school.

2 A famous actor opened the show.
The show _____ a famous actor.

3 The school spends a lot of money on new books.
A lot of money _____ on new books.

4 They don't sell crisps in the school shop now.
Crisps _____ in the school shop now.

5 The teacher didn't tell us about the school trip.
We _____ about the school trip.

6 A problem with the electrical system caused the fire.
The fire _____ a problem with the electrical system.

3 Complete the conversations with the passive form of the verbs in the box.

encourage	not include	not invite
send	steal	tell

A: Is this a good college?
B: Yes. The teachers are good, and everyone ¹ _____ to work hard.

A: Where's your bike?
B: It ² _____ yesterday! I'm so annoyed!

A: How do you usually get your exam results?
B: They ³ _____ by email, or you can look on the college website.

A: Have we got an exam tomorrow?
B: Yes! We ⁴ _____ about it last week!

A: I was surprised that Dan wasn't at the party on Saturday.
B: Me too. He ⁵ _____ for some reason.

A: £50 seems cheap for the school trip to London.
B: Yes, but remember food ⁶ _____ in that price.

For each question, choose the correct answer.

Teacher Jack Greening talks about setting up a school photography club

Last year the headteacher came and asked me to start a photography club. Our school already has lots of fantastic sports clubs, which is great, but not all students like sport. My classroom's decorated with photos I've taken, but they're not exactly works of art and I wasn't sure I was a good enough photographer to teach others. But I wanted to run a school club and the headteacher promised money for cameras, memory cards, tripods, and so on – so I said yes.

There were so many things to consider before I started, and I knew my colleagues were too busy to help. Should the club be for students with experience? Should it be for the whole school, or only some year-groups? Above all, what did I want to achieve? To enter student competitions, or just to take photos for the school website? In the end I decided my aim was for beginners to have fun with photography. I held the sessions in a science lab where we could lock stuff that we needed for the club in a cupboard.

About fifteen students came to the first session. Some of them were clearly only there to be with their mates. Still, I got them all to take photos of each other. We put these on the screen and the keen students chatted about the good and not so good points. I hadn't expected them to have so many good ideas about what they could do better next time.

The second week, most of the students came back, and another twenty-five joined. I had to ask the headteacher to get another teacher to share the sessions. Colleagues heard students talking about the club in lessons and advised me about things to do with students, including taking them to a famous photographer's exhibition. A year later, and I've no regrets about starting this club. The students have worked hard on their photography. Some clearly have a natural ability, which helps. I've already planned next year's photographic projects, but our school cameras are quite basic. To take really amazing photos, the students need a more advanced one of their own – that's the best way to improve.

1 How did Jack feel when he was first asked to set up the photography club?
- **A** stressed because he had enough to do already
- **B** worried by the lack of photography equipment
- **C** anxious about his photography skills
- **D** disappointed as he wanted to run a sports club

2 In the second paragraph, what does Jack say was the most important thing for him to decide?
- **A** how much help he would need
- **B** which students the club was for
- **C** where sessions would take place
- **D** what the purpose of the club was

3 What surprised Jack at the club's first session?
- **A** how many different types of students took part
- **B** how good most of the students' photos were
- **C** how well students could discuss their photos
- **D** how serious all the students were about photography

4 How did Jack's colleagues react when they heard about his club?
- **A** They suggested some possible activities.
- **B** They offered to run the sessions with Jack.
- **C** They asked Jack for advice about their own clubs.
- **D** They recommended some students to join the club.

5 What might Jack say to the parents of students in his photography club?
- **A** 'I've enjoyed helping your children this year, but in order to make further progress they now need to do a proper photography course.'
- **B** 'Some of your children had the advantage of previous experience using cameras, but they've all made great progress.'
- **C** 'If your children are interested in becoming better photographers, encourage them by taking them to see photography exhibitions.'
- **D** 'To be a great photographer requires talent and lots of practice, but it helps if your children have good cameras too.'

Complete the passive sentences.

1 Someone has broken a window in one of the classrooms.
   A window in one of the classrooms ....

2 Someone is repairing the school minibus at the moment.
   The school minibus .... at the moment.

3 They had announced the winner two weeks earlier.
   The winner .... two weeks earlier.

4 They should clean the classrooms every day.
   The classrooms .... every day.

5 Everyone must complete their project by Friday.
   All projects .... by Friday.

6 You can't use dictionaries in the exam.
   Dictionaries .... in the exam.

LISTENING

1 14 **Listen to a radio discussion about learning. Which sentence best summarises the discussion?**

A Stella Bradshaw talks about her own experiences of learning different skills through her life.

B Stella Bradshaw discusses which new skills are the best ones to learn as an adult.

C Stella Bradshaw talks about the advantages of continuing to learn new things as an adult.

2 14 **Listen again. Decide if the sentences are true or false.**

1 Stella wrote her book because of her own experiences.

2 Mavis Bowman left school because she wasn't keen on learning when she was a teenager.

3 According to Stella, older people don't learn as quickly as younger people.

4 Stella says the main reason for learning new things as an adult is that it makes life more interesting.

5 Kevin learned to ride a bike quite easily when he was 28.

6 Stella's advice to listeners is to avoid things that they found very difficult when they were younger.

SPEAKING

1 Match the sentence halves about people's likes and dislikes at school.

1 I love ....
2 I'm not very interested ....
3 When I was younger, I was quite good ....
4 I'm bored ....
5 I can't ....
6 I'm quite keen ....

a at maths.
b stand economics!
c chemistry and biology.
d on English.
e by physics.
f in history.

2 Complete what the people say with one word in each gap.

1 I .... mind biology, but I hate physics!
2 I've always been terrible .... art.
3 I really don't like history. I .... it really dull!
4 I'm fascinated .... different countries, so I love geography.
5 I .... bear IT – it's my worst subject!
6 When I was younger, I .... maths was boring, but now I know how important it is.

WRITING

1 Complete the email with the words in the box.

could	dear	enquire	finally
know	let	look	sincerely

¹ .... Mr Green,

I am writing to ² .... about the drama course at Homewood Hall.
Please ³ .... you tell me how long the course lasts? I would also like to ⁴ .... if all the equipment is provided.
⁵ .... , please could you ⁶ .... me know if there are still vacancies on the course?
I ⁷ .... forward to hearing from you.

Yours ⁸ .... ,
Emma Ashton

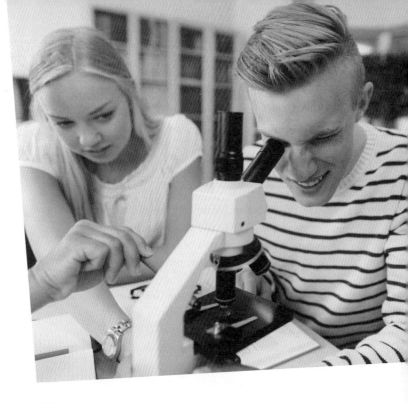

2 Complete the indirect questions. Use the word in brackets.

1 Where does the course take place?
   I'd ....
   .... place. (know)
2 Is food included in the price?
   Please could ....
   .... the price. (tell)
3 What should I bring with me?
   Please ....
   .... bring with me. (let)
4 Can I get to the college by bus?
   Please could ....
   .... the college by bus. (tell)
5 Is there a minimum age for students?
   I'd ....
   .... a minimum age for students. (know)
6 Is the course fully booked?
   Please ....
   .... fully booked. (let)

VOCABULARY

1 Read the clues and complete the puzzle. Then write the mystery word in the shaded column.

1 the place where boats arrive and leave from

2 a large boat that carries passengers and sometimes cars

3 a situation when the cars and lorries on the road cannot move forwards (2 words)

4 a journey by plane

5 the place where a train leaves from at a railway station

6 a situation when a train, bus or plane is late

7 a place where you can buy fuel for your car (2 words)

Mystery word: ....

Clue: It's important, so don't lose it! (2 words)

Crossword grid:
- 1 P _ _ (with P, A, N, S shaded column starting)
- 2 F _ _
- 3 T _ _ _ _ _ J _ _
- N
- 4 F _ _ _
- 5 P _ _ F _ _ M
- 6 D _ _ _
- S
- 7 P _ _ _ _ _ T _ _ _ _ _

2 Complete the advice about flying with the words in the box.

| airline | business class | cabin staff | check-in |
| cockpit | departure lounge | flight attendant | gate |

TIPS FOR STRESS-FREE FLYING

1 When you buy your ticket, think about paying a bit more for a .... seat – they're a lot more comfortable!

2 Make sure you know which .... you are travelling with before you get to the airport.

3 When you get to the airport, go straight to .... to collect your boarding pass.

4 Wait in the .... until your plane is ready to board.

5 When your plane is ready to board, go to the correct ....

6 The .... will greet you as you get on the plane.

7 If you have any problems during your flight, speak to a ....

8 Remember, it is against the law to try to enter the .... where the pilot is sitting!

3 Complete the comments about travel experiences opposite with the correct form of a phrasal verb. Use *get* and the correct particle from the box.

| around | back | into | off | out of | to |

What's your best, worst or funniest travel experience?

We'd love to know!

JennaJ
Last year, my friend and I **1** .... a tuk tuk taxi in India to take us up a steep hill. But the taxi was so old, it couldn't get up the hill! In the end, we **2** .... the taxi and walked!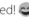

Sam88
I once chose to visit a small village in Italy because there was a train station there and I liked the name. But when I **3** .... the train, I found there was nothing there except a few houses – and no more trains until the next day!

LucyLu
My cousin and I were visiting the Greek islands last summer and hired bikes to **4** .... Unfortunately, I fell off and ended up in hospital!

James123
I once decided to walk from the airport to my hotel, to save money. It took me five hours, and I was exhausted when I finally **5** .... my hotel!

TomG
I was on a flight into London last year, but there was a storm so they took us to Hamburg. I finally **6** .... home 26 hours later!

GRAMMAR

1 Complete the zero conditional sentences with the correct form of the verbs in brackets. There is one verb in each group that you don't need.

1 When I .... on holiday, I .... to travel by plane. (prefer / go / arrive)

2 Everyone .... if the train .... late. (be / complain / get)

3 I always .... better when I .... to work. (walk / like / feel)

4 You .... a lot of money if you .... your bike to get around the city. (use / get / save)

5 If you .... your tickets in advance, they .... much cheaper. (be / cost / buy)

2 Complete the dialogues with the correct form of the verbs to make first conditional sentences.

1 **A:** Shall we walk to the cinema?
　B: No – it's raining! We .... (get) wet if we .... (walk)!

2 **A:** What .... (we / do) if Jack .... (not / be) at the airport to meet us?
　B: We'll call him – I've got his number.

3 **A:** Is it time to go?
　B: Yes, and you need to hurry up. You .... (miss) your plane unless you .... (leave) now!

4 **A:** I'll pay for the coffees.
　B: Thanks. If you .... (pay) for these, I .... (buy) you a sandwich on the flight!

5 **A:** Are you going to get the train to Oxford tomorrow?
　B: No, I .... (go) by car, unless the roads .... (be) too busy.

3 Complete the second sentence so it has a similar meaning to the first. Use the word in brackets.

1 We'll only go to the beach if it's sunny.
We won't .... sunny. (unless)

2 We'll go to the concert unless the tickets are too expensive.
We .... too expensive. (won't)

3 If I pass all my exams, my parents will buy me a car.
My parents .... I pass all my exams. (unless)

4 We won't get a taxi unless there are no buses.
We'll .... buses. (only)

5 I'll buy some shoes if I see some that I like.
I won't .... some that I like. (any)

6 I'll come to the party unless I have a lot of homework.
I .... a lot of homework. (if)

4 Complete the sentences with the zero or first conditional form of the verb in brackets.

1 I always .... (walk) through the park when it .... (is) sunny.

2 I .... (call) you from the station later if there .... (be) any delays with the trains.

3 If I .... (see) Rob this afternoon, I .... (tell) him you're looking for him.

4 Tara always .... (get) annoyed if the bus .... (be) late!

5 If I .... (go) to work early, there .... (be) always plenty of seats on the train.

6 What .... (you / do) if your car .... (break down) on the motorway tomorrow?

5 Complete the text with the correct second conditional form of the verbs.

SHOULD WE SIMPLY STOP USING PLASTIC?

A lot of people think the world ¹ .... (be) a better place if we ² .... (stop) using plastic. But is it really that simple? For example, if we ³ .... (use) glass bottles for things like milk, they ⁴ .... (be) heavier. If lorries ⁵ .... (have to) carry more weight, they ⁶ .... (use) more fuel, and this ⁷ .... (cause) more pollution. Also, if we ⁸ .... (not / have) plastic for things like bags and phone cases, companies ⁹ .... (make) more things out of leather, so we ¹⁰ .... (have) more animals, and they ¹¹ .... (need) more water and food. A lot of clothes use plastic too, and if we ¹² .... (change) to more natural materials, we ¹³ .... (grow) more cotton, which ¹⁴ .... (use) a lot of natural resources. As you can see, the *problem* of plastic is simple, but the solutions are much more difficult!

6 Complete the sentences with the correct form of the verbs in brackets.

1 If I .... (have) lots of money, I would travel all around the world!

2 Our old car never starts easily when the weather .... (be) cold.

3 I'll go for a pizza with you on Saturday if I .... (have) enough money.

4 If I .... (eat) chocolate, it gives me a headache.

5 If the trains were more comfortable, more people .... (use) them.

6 If you tell me what time your train arrives tomorrow, I .... (come) to the station to meet you.

7 I'll ride my bike to college tomorrow unless I .... (have) a lot of books to carry.

8 You would be much fitter if you .... (walk) to work every day!

READING

1 Read the article. Which sentence best sums up what the article says?

A Plastic rubbish on beaches isn't a big problem yet, but it will be in a few years.

B Plastic rubbish on beaches is a big problem, but people are finding creative solutions.

C The problem of plastic rubbish on beaches is getting worse, and the government should do something about it.

A SEA OF PLASTIC

A recent storm in the south west of England brought an unexpected problem – large amounts of plastic rubbish on the beaches. The oceans are full of plastic, and when a storm moves the water more than usual, it can also lift this rubbish from the bottom of the sea and move it to the shore. It is clearly a big problem, but some people are now taking action themselves.

The power of volunteers

In one town, a group of local people have decided to clean up their beach themselves. Although they are all volunteers, so they aren't paid, they spend every weekend down on the shore, collecting as much rubbish as they can. They put it into different bags, depending on the type. They sell anything valuable, recycle as much as possible, and leave the rest to be taken away as rubbish. They also encourage tourists who use the beach to pick up five pieces of rubbish before they leave.

From rubbish to art

One family is using art to make people think about the problem of plastic in the oceans. Sara and John Bailey, together with their two children, regularly collect rubbish from the beach near their home and use it to create works of art. Sara says they have great fun together choosing which things to use and thinking of clever ways to use them. The works of art go into local shops, and the money they make from them pays for any materials that they need.

Boats to collect more rubbish

A bigger project is using plastic from the oceans to create useful products for local people. The project, which receives financial help from the government, collects plastic from the beach. It sends it to a local factory, where it is recycled and made into kayaks, or small boats. These kayaks go back to local people at no cost, and people can then use them to spend time on the sea collecting more plastic.

Although governments clearly need to take action to deal with the problem of plastic in the oceans, it seems that individuals and local groups can also be a big part of the solution.

2 Read the article again. Which project are the sentences about? Write **V** (volunteer plastic pickers), **A** (the art project) or **K** (the kayak project).

1 They sort the rubbish that they collect. ....

2 They give the things that they make to local people. ....

3 The project receives money to pay for the work. ....

4 They enjoy the work that they do. ....

5 They try to persuade other people to join in and help. ....

6 They sell the things that they make. ....

PUSH YOURSELF /B2

15 Listen to four people talking about some new cycle paths in their city. Choose the correct opinion for each person.

1 A They're good, but they're quite dangerous.

B They're good, and safe to use at any time.

C They're only useful during the day.

2 A They're not very good, and the signs aren't easy to see.

B They're excellent, and you can easily see where you're going.

C They're quite good, but difficult to follow.

3 A They aren't good at all.

B They're quite good, but there should be more of them.

C They're very good, and they should advertise them more.

4 A They're not useful because there aren't enough of them.

B They're useful, but they're sometimes too crowded.

C They're very useful, especially in the mornings.

🎧 16 For each question, choose the correct answer.

1 You will hear two friends talking about a new airport. They both think that
- **A** the location is very convenient.
- **B** the recycling facilities are great.
- **C** the signs are clear.

2 You will hear a woman telling her brother about her new electric bicycle.
How does she feel about it?
- **A** not sure about how long it will last
- **B** worried about where to leave it at college
- **C** embarrassed about going to college on it

3 You will hear two colleagues talking about travelling to work.
Why does the man prefer taking the train?
- **A** He can do some work before arriving at his office.
- **B** There's nowhere to park near where he works.
- **C** Driving home in the evening takes too long.

4 You will hear two friends talking about getting to the airport.
They agree to
- **A** make a decision after doing some research.
- **B** travel to the airport together.
- **C** wait for each other at the entrance.

5 You will hear two neighbours talking about traffic in the town.
The man thinks that
- **A** the roads are confusing for visitors.
- **B** fewer cars are already coming into the town.
- **C** more changes are needed to solve the problems.

6 You will hear two friends talking about recycling.
The woman says that she
- **A** uses more glass than plastic.
- **B** finds it hard to avoid using plastic.
- **C** is careful which types of plastic she uses.

SPEAKING

1 Read the sentences which speculate about things you can see in a picture. Choose the correct meaning for each sentence.

1 I think the two boys must be brothers.
- **A** I'm sure they are brothers.
- **B** It's possible that they are brothers.

2 They might be on holiday.
- **A** I'm sure they are on holiday.
- **B** It's possible that they are on holiday.

3 It may not be her car.
- **A** I'm sure it isn't her car.
- **B** It's possible that it isn't her car.

4 It can't be summer.
- **A** It's possible that it's not summer.
- **B** I'm sure it isn't summer.

5 It could be some kind of meat.
- **A** It's possible that it's some kind of meat.
- **B** I'm sure it's some kind of meat.

6 It can't be in Africa.
- **A** I'm sure it's in Africa.
- **B** It isn't possible that it's in Africa.

2 Complete the second sentence so it has a similar meaning to the first. Use a modal of speculation.

1 I'm sure it's a rescue boat.
It _____ a rescue boat.

2 I guess it's possible that he's a teacher.
I guess he _____ a teacher.

3 I'm sure she isn't very old.
She _____ very old.

4 It's possible that he isn't pleased with his grades.
He _____ pleased with his grades.

WRITING

1 Complete the sentences with the correct narrative tenses of the verbs.

Last Thursday evening, I **¹**had sat / was sitting in the *Top Pizza* restaurant on West Street, waiting for some friends. The waiter **²**came / was coming over and asked if I wanted to order. 'No, not yet,' I **³**replied / was replying. I **⁴**looked / was looking at the time on my phone. It was 7.45. Where were they? We **⁵**agreed / had agreed to meet at 7.30. While **⁶**I thought / was thinking about what to do next, my phone **⁷**rang / was ringing. 'Where are you?' my friend Callum **⁸**asked / had asked. 'We're all waiting for you in the *Top Pizza* restaurant on Bridge Street!'

2 Rewrite the direct speech sentences with the correct punctuation.

1 nice to meet you she said

_____

2 where are you going he asked

_____

3 go away she shouted

_____

4 come with me he whispered quietly

_____

3 Choose the best verbs for the direct speech.

1 'Don't make too much noise,' he whispered / cried.
2 'Are you feeling better?' she asked / said.
3 'The money has gone,' he said / told me.
4 'You can't come in!' I asked / shouted.
5 'Hello!' he told / called.

11 A GREAT LOCATION

VOCABULARY

1 Complete the words in the people's descriptions of their homes.

I live in a ¹t_____ r____ c____d h_____ e near the city centre. It's quite small, but it's warm and ²c_____y. It's an ³o____d-f_____ n____d house, not a modern one, but I like it!

I live in quite a big house in the ⁴s____b_____bs, about five miles from the city centre. It's a ⁵t_____-s_____r____y house, with an upstairs and a downstairs. It's a ⁶b_____d n____w house, so everything in it is very modern. It's quite close to my school, which is very ⁷c____nv__n_____t.

I live in a tall ⁸b _____k of f_____s in the city centre, near the ⁹b__s__n_____s d____st_____t where my dad works. We live on the ¹⁰t____p f_____r, so we have a great view of the city!

2 Complete the house and home quiz.

1 Where can you heat water?
A a kettle B a cabinet C a tap

2 Where do you hang clothes?
A a chest of drawers B a wardrobe C a cabinet

3 What do you put on your bed to keep warm?
A a rug B a cushion C a duvet

4 Where do you put rubbish?
A a chest of drawers B a rug C a bin

5 Where can you get water from?
A a bin B a rug C a tap

6 What do you put on the floor to look nice?
A a rug B a cushion C a duvet

7 Where can you keep things in a bathroom?
A a chest of drawers B a bin C a cabinet

8 What do you put on a chair to make it more comfortable?
A a cushion B a rug C a duvet

3 Complete the list of problems with a new flat.

The mirror on the bathroom
_____ _____ _____ _____ is cracked, so you can't see yourself very well.

The _____ _____ isn't working properly, so the flat is cold.

There's a horrible stain on the _____ on the hall floor.

The _____ _____ from the sofa are missing. It looks odd without them.

One _____ _____ _____ and one chest of drawers aren't enough for two people. We need more space to store our clothes.

The tap on the kitchen _____ _____ _____ needs fixing. We can't turn it off completely.

GRAMMAR

1 Choose the correct relative pronouns. In one sentence, both are correct.

1 Jan showed me the house *which / where* she lives.
2 The people *that / whose* I share a flat with are all really friendly.
3 This is the flat *which / who* they want to buy.
4 The friend *who / whose* flat I stayed at is called Ed.
5 The people *who / which* live next door are very nice.
6 This was a time *when / which* most people lived together in big family groups.
7 I need to make a list of all the people *who / that* I'm inviting to the housewarming party.
8 The sofa *that / who* we bought was too big.

2 Complete the sentences with the relative clauses.

which we looked at	which is near the city centre
which is annoying	who lives in London
who owns our flat	

1 Some of the houses _____ were too expensive for us to rent.
2 The person _____ also owns five other flats.
3 My friend Tom, _____, is mad about skateboarding.
4 Our flat, _____, is quite small and modern.
5 It takes me nearly an hour to get to school, _____.

3 Look at the relative clauses in exercise 2 again. Are they defining or non-defining? Write D or ND. In which two sentences can you use *that* instead of *which* or *who*?

1 _____   3 _____   5 _____
2 _____   4 _____

You can use *that* in sentences _____ and _____.

4 Read the blog post. Write the numbers of the three bold relative pronouns that you can leave out.

This is the first week in my new flat, and I love it! For a start, it's close to a big park, ¹**which** is great! It's also close to the school ²**where** I'll go in September. And my friend Sam, ³**who** I've known all my life, lives just around the corner. What could be better? The bedroom ⁴**that** I've chosen is quite big. All the things ⁵**which** I brought with me from our old flat fit in easily. The other people ⁶**who** live on our floor also seem very nice. One guy ⁷**who** I've met likes the same computer games as me, so I'm sure we'll be friends!

_____

5 Join the sentences using a relative clause. Sometimes more than one relative pronoun is possible. Remember to add commas if the clause is non-defining.

1 This is the swimming pool. I use it in the summer.
This is the swimming pool _____
in the summer.

2 The new flats are expensive. They are building them in the business district.
The new flats _____
_____ expensive.

3 My friend Sam lives in the suburbs. He's really sporty.
My friend Sam _____
lives in the suburbs.

4 Manchester is a great city. I live there.
Manchester _____
a great city.

5 You can use these tennis courts for free. It's amazing!
You can use these tennis courts for free _____
_____ amazing!

6 I have met some new people. They are all very nice.
The new people _____
all very nice.

6 Rewrite the sentences using *have* or *get*.

1 Someone took our photo next to the fountain.
We _____
next to the fountain. (had)

2 I need to ask someone to fix my phone this weekend.
I need to _____
this weekend. (get)

3 Has someone cut your hair?
Have _____ ? (had)

4 You can ask someone to deliver your shopping to your home.
You can _____
to your home. (have)

5 It's a good idea to ask someone to check your running style before you buy new trainers.
It's a good idea to _____
_____ before you buy new trainers. (get)

LISTENING

1 🔊 17 Listen to three young people talking about where they live in London. What have they all found?

A a clever way to meet new people and make friends
B a different way to travel to and from work cheaply
C an unusual way to live cheaply in the city

2 🔊 17 Listen again. Which person, Ewan, Daisy, or Andy …

1 has met other young people that they have something in common with? _____
2 doesn't have a very good bathroom? _____
3 had some problems when they first moved into their home? _____
4 is free to make changes to their home? _____
5 is going to leave their home soon? _____
6 lives close to their job? _____

For each question, choose the correct answer.

Houses that can turn around

Would you like to live in a house that follows the direction of the sun in winter and provides shade when it's really hot? This is fast becoming a **(1)** _____, as more architects around the world are designing buildings that turn around. Known as 'rotating houses', these homes are the **(2)** _____ solution for anyone who's ever **(3)** _____ like waking up to a different view from their bedroom window. And many of these houses are controlled by motors no bigger than washing machines.

Luke Everingham lives in a rotating house built with glass, metal and natural **(4)** _____ such as wood. The house is an eight-sided shape and there are eight rooms inside. Luke uses a remote control in the living room to **(5)** _____ his house turn. It takes thirty minutes to complete a full circle, so you can't **(6)** _____ it's turning unless you focus on an object outside.

1	**A** fact	**B** truth	**C** reality	**D** habit
2	**A** great	**B** perfect	**C** good	**D** fantastic
3	**A** thought	**B** dreamt	**C** wanted	**D** felt
4	**A** materials	**B** ingredients	**C** contents	**D** parts
5	**A** make	**B** cause	**C** achieve	**D** force
6	**A** find	**B** compare	**C** tell	**D** learn

PUSH YOURSELF /B2

Complete the advertisements for flats to rent with adjectives.

For rent
A large double room in a
1s _____ n _____ g
modern flat in a quiet
2r _____ d _____ t _____ l
area. The room is fully
3f _____ n _____ s _____ d, and
all bills are included in the rent.

For rent
A **4**d _____ l _____ t _____ l
two-bedroom flat in the city centre.
Very **5**s p _____ c _____ s,
and with a large balcony.

For rent
A **6**u _____ i _____ e three-bedroom
flat in the business district. It has
a **7**l _____ x _____ r _____ s
modern bathroom and
8p _____ c _____ r _____ s _____ e
views over the historic town centre.

SPEAKING

1 Match the beginnings and ends of the expressions you can use for showing that you are surprised. Sometimes there is more than one possible answer. There is one ending you don't need.

1 No
2 You're
3 How
4 Wow!
5 Really?

a incredible!
b I'd never have guessed that.
c way!
d joking!
e the way!
f That's unbelievable!

2 Choose the correct words to complete the description.

> We're staying in an amazing holiday flat, right by the beach. There's one big room for living in and there's, **1**____, a big glass door which opens out onto a **2**____ large balcony, where you can sit and see the sea. There's a big games room, with a table tennis table and **3**____ like that. There's **4**____ outdoor cooker where you can barbecue and cook your meals outside. And there's a shed outside with things for the beach – surfboards, small boats, those **5**____ of things. Down by the beach, there's **6**____ of natural swimming pool in the rocks, where the water's really warm – perfect!

	A		**B**		**C**	
1	A	kind	B	like	C	sort
2	A	sort	B	types of	C	kind of
3	A	stuff	B	kinds	C	sorts
4	A	a type of	B	a kind	C	like
5	A	stuff	B	like	C	kinds
6	A	type of	B	a sort	C	kind

WRITING

1 Choose the correct words to complete the sentences you can use in an email.

1 Thank you *of / for* your email.
2 Congratulations *on / for* your exam results.
3 I'm *afraid / scared* I can't come to the party.
4 Perhaps I *would / could* visit you in July?
5 I'm looking forward to *see / seeing* you soon.
6 Write *back / me* soon.

2 Complete the email with words from the box. There are some words you don't need.

> best   dear   fortunately   get   getting   look
> looking   love   perhaps   possible   unfortunately

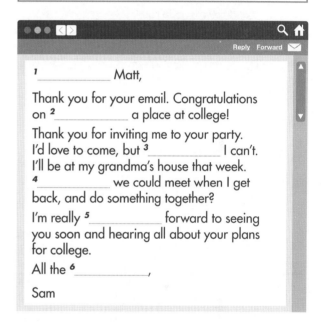

1_____ Matt,

Thank you for your email. Congratulations on **2**_____ a place at college!

Thank you for inviting me to your party. I'd love to come, but **3**_____ I can't. I'll be at my grandma's house that week.

4_____ we could meet when I get back, and do something together?

I'm really **5**_____ forward to seeing you soon and hearing all about your plans for college.

All the **6**_____,

Sam

12 THE PERFECT JOB

VOCABULARY

1 **Read the clues and write the jobs.**

1
> Call me if you have a problem with your taps.
> p _ _ _ _ _ _ b _ _ r

2
> I'm good at maths, and you can trust me with your money! a _ _ _ _ _ _ _ _ _ _ t _ _ _ _ t

3
> I help people when they have committed crimes and have to go to court. l _ _ _ _ _ y _ _ r

4
> You can come to me if you're ill and need medicines or tablets. p _ _ _ _ _ r m _ _ c _ _ _ _ _ t

5
> Call me if the lights in your house suddenly go out!
> e _ _ _ _ _ _ _ _ t r _ _ c _ _ _ _ n

2 **What's the best job for each young person?**

architect	astronaut	lecturer
politician	programmer	

1 **John:** I think computers are amazing – and you can make them do some really cool things.
   ....

2 **Amy:** I enjoy teaching, but I'd like to teach older students, not young kids. ....

3 **Eva:** There are a lot of problems in the world, and I'd like to do something to help.
   ....

4 **Noah:** I want to see the world – from as far away as possible! ....

5 **Elsa:** I love buildings, especially modern ones with interesting designs. ....

3 **Choose the correct adjective.**

1 Maria never gets angry, even if she has to show me how to do something three times! (*creative / patient / reliable*)

2 Dan comes up with some amazing new ideas! (*organised / creative / flexible*)

3 Rob is really good at solving problems – he's so clever! (*intelligent / reliable / friendly*)

4 Abi never seems stressed, even when we're really busy. (*calm / intelligent / creative*)

5 Ollie always says hello to other people, and asks how they are. (*flexible / friendly / organised*)

6 Eva is never late, and she always finishes her work on time. (*creative / flexible / reliable*)

7 Paolo plans his work carefully, and always knows exactly what he needs to do. (*friendly / intelligent / organised*)

8 Jeni is always happy to change her plans if a situation changes. (*reliable / flexible / friendly*)

4 **Complete the tips with the words in the box.**

co-workers	director	employee
employer	freelancer	line manager
personal assistant	sales staff	

HOW TO BE HAPPY AND SUCCESSFUL AT WORK

1 Be cheerful and polite to the people you work with – your .... don't want to work with someone who's always complaining!

2 If you have any problems, the first person to talk to is your .... – this is the person who is directly above you in the company.

3 If you need to talk to an important person in the company, don't call them directly – talk to their .... first, who can probably arrange an appointment for you.

4 Remember you are part of a team at work – you aren't the only .... in the company!

5 If you have an idea for a new product, talk to the .... – their job is to sell things and they will know if people will want to buy your idea.

6 If you are ambitious, be patient – it takes about twenty years to reach the top and become the .... of a company!

7 Always respect the company you work for. Remember, the company is your .... and pays you each month!

8 If you really hate working for a company, you can always leave and become a ...., working for yourself.

5 Complete the information on a careers website with the words in the box.

certificate communication doctorate good at
good with master's problem-solving

Being a plumber is a great job if you like working with your hands. You can start a training course straight after high school, and at the end you will get a
¹_____ to show you are able to do the job. You must be friendly and
²_____ people, and sometimes you have to work out the best way to do something, so you need ³_____ skills.

To become a university lecturer, you need a bachelor's and a ⁴_____ degree, and finally you have to spend three more years studying for a ⁵_____. Apart from these qualifications, you also need to be
⁶_____ presenting information, and of course you also need excellent
⁷_____ skills so you can explain your ideas to students.

GRAMMAR

1 Choose the correct modal verbs.

A: ¹*Could / Must* I borrow your pen, please?

B: Yes, of course you ²*could / can*.

A: ³*May / Couldn't* I speak to Chris, please?

B: No, I'm sorry, you ⁴*can't / couldn't* speak to him at the moment. He's in a meeting.

A: ⁵*Must / Can* I eat my lunch at my desk?

B: Yes, that's fine, but you ⁶*couldn't / mustn't* spill food on your laptop!

A: ⁷*Are we allowed to / Must* we finish early on a Friday?

B: Yes, but you ⁸*couldn't / can't* leave before 4 p.m.

2 Look at the school rules from a school in 1900. Then complete the sentences with *had to* or the correct form of *be allowed to* and the verbs in brackets.

All children must be in school by 8.30 a.m.

Uniform is black skirts for girls and black short trousers for boys under 11, long trousers for boys over 11.

Coats may be kept on in the classroom in cold weather.

In 1900, the children ¹_____
(be) in school by 8.30 a.m. Boys under 11 years old
²_____ (wear) long trousers.
Girls ³_____ (wear) black skirts. They ⁴_____ (keep)
their coats on in the classroom in cold weather.

3 Read the sentences and choose the correct meanings.

1 My parents usually let me stay up late at the weekend.
  A I can't stay up late at the weekend.
  B I am allowed to stay up late at the weekend.

2 My parents make me do my homework before I can play on the computer.
  A I have to do my homework first.
  B I am not allowed to do my homework first.

3 My brother didn't let me borrow his bike last weekend.
  A I was allowed to borrow his bike.
  B I wasn't allowed to borrow his bike.

4 When I was younger, my parents made me help around the house.
  A I was allowed to help around the house.
  B I had to help around the house.

4 Complete the second sentence so it has a similar meaning to the first. Use the word in brackets.

1 My parents say I have to keep my bedroom tidy.
My parents _____
my bedroom tidy. (make)

2 Our teachers say we can't use our phones in class.
Our teachers _____
our phones in class. (let)

3 Her boss didn't let her go home early.
She _____
home early. (allowed)

4 My mum made me go to bed early when I was young.
I _____
early when I was young. (had)

5 Our teacher sometimes says we're allowed to look online for information.
Our teacher sometimes _____
online for information. (lets)

6 You mustn't park here.
You _____ here. (allowed)

Complete the sentences with a modal verb and *be able to*. Sometimes more than one modal verb is possible.

1 Look, he's right there, on the other side of the room. I'm sure you can see him!
You _____ him!

2 It will be possible for you to talk to her tomorrow.
You _____ to her tomorrow.

3 It's possible that we can buy our uniforms online.
We _____
our uniforms online.

4 It's wrong that people can't camp here.
People _____ here.

5 I don't have many qualifications, so I can't get a job.
If I had more qualifications, I _____
a job.

READING

1 Match the jobs with the meanings.

1 farmer _____ **2** chef _____ **3** barista _____ **4** childcare assistant _____

a someone who cooks food in a restaurant
b someone who uses a machine to make coffee in a café
c someone who looks after young children while their parents are working
d someone who grows crops and keeps animals to produce food

2 Read the article. Match the correct job with each paragraph.

A pharmacist   **C** farmer   **E** barista
B childcare assistant   **D** chef   **F** tour guide

ARE ROBOTS ? TAKING OUR JOBS

HOME   NEWS   ABOUT

Some people worry that robots will carry out a lot more of our jobs in the future. But is this true? Which jobs can robots do, and which jobs will they never be able to do?

1 ....
In some cafés, coffee is already served by a robot, or a robot arm at least. The arm picks up a cup, moves it to the coffee machine and presses the buttons to produce a perfect cup of coffee in about 30 seconds, which is faster than a human. Another advantage is that the robot never needs a break, and it doesn't get angry with difficult customers!

2 ....
On the other hand, if you go into a restaurant kitchen, you will find the staff are still one hundred percent human. Cooking is a creative activity, and no one has managed to produce a creative robot yet. Experts also believe that robots will never be able to cook delicious food because they can't smell or taste it.

3 ....
At one university in the United States, there is already a robot which prepares medicines for patients to collect. Doctors order the medicines online, then the robot puts the correct tablets into bottles and prints the labels. So far, the robot

hasn't got anything wrong, and it is better than a human pharmacist because it can check more easily whether two medicines might not work well together.

4 ....
Robots can teach some things such as languages, but experts say they will never be able to look after young children. Young children need human contact, and they need people who can understand them. Robots can be taught to recognise behaviours, such as when someone laughs or gets angry, but they will never know when someone is upset or lonely, or scared.

5 ....
The job of growing food includes a lot of routine work which robots can definitely do. This year, a British university has completed a project to grow a complete crop hands-free, using only machines to plant it, look after it, and pick it. They now want to work towards running a whole farm using just machines.

6 ....
We now spend more and more of our working and home lives with machines. Research shows that when we're on holiday, however, we want more human contact. People who know a place well can help us to enjoy new places and new adventures in a way that is exciting and challenging for us. For this reason, humans will always be needed for this job.

3 Read the article again. Which job is each sentence about?

1 There are plans to do more work using robots in the future. ....
2 Robots are quicker and they don't get tired. ....
3 Customers want a real person to help them gain more from an experience. ....
4 This robot hasn't made a mistake yet. ....
5 Robots can't do this job because they don't have all the senses that humans have. ....
6 Robots can't do this job because they don't understand how people are feeling. ....

🎧 18 **For each question, choose the correct answer.**

1 What is the woman's job now?

A **B** **C**

2 Which benefit does the man's company offer staff?

A **B** **C**

3 Who works in the sales department?

A **B** **C**

4 Where does the man work?

A **B** **C**

5 What does the woman like best about her job?

A **B** **C**

6 What was the man's career ambition when he was a child?

A **B** **C**

7 Who is the woman's sister?

A **B** **C**

SPEAKING

1 **Complete the conversations with words from the box. There are some words you don't need.**

> agree   disagree   exactly   I'd
> I'm   perhaps   right   sorry

1 **A:** I think that politicians should be paid more.
   B: _____ , but I don't agree. They get quite enough already!
2 **A:** We need to encourage more people to become teachers.
   B: _____ ! We really need more teachers.
3 **A:** Nurses should get the same salary as doctors.
   B: I'm afraid I _____ . Doctors have to train for many years.
4 **A:** Firefighters do a very dangerous job.
   B: Yes, you're right. _____ agree with that.

2 **Choose the correct expression.**

1 **A:** I think George would be a brilliant politician!
   B: *Sorry, but I don't agree. / Yes, you're right.* He really wants to make people's lives better.
2 **A:** I think working as a programmer would be fun.
   B: *Exactly! / I don't think that's true.* I think a lot of their work must be really quite boring!
3 **A:** It's easy to become an electrician!
   B: *I agree with you. / I'm afraid I disagree.* You need to do a lot of training, actually.
4 **A:** I think it must be amazing to be an astronaut.
   B: *Perhaps, but it's not all fun. / I'd agree with that.* It must be great to look down at the Earth!

WRITING

Complete the job advertisement.

> applicants   application   full-time   must
> opportunity   qualifications   should be able

MAGIC ASSISTANT

Why not become a magic assistant? This is a great
1 _____ for someone who enjoys being on the stage and wants to try something different! This is a **2** _____ job, starting next month.

3 _____ should be 18 years old and in good health. They **4** _____ to make decisions quickly and keep smiling when things go wrong. They **5** _____ be brave and able to hide their fear! There are no **6** _____ necessary for this job – we will consider anyone who loves magic shows!

Please send your **7** _____ to jojomagic@magicshows.org.

13 GET INVOLVED!

VOCABULARY

1 Complete what the people say about sport with the correct form of the verbs in brackets. There is one verb in each group that you don't need.

I decided last year that I should ¹_____ a new sport, so I ²_____ my local tennis club. I love it! I'm much healthier now and I even ³_____ the club in matches from time to time!
(*hold / join / represent / take up*)

I do athletics, but just for fun. I don't often ⁴_____ in competitions. I don't want to take it too seriously because I also enjoy ⁵_____ at the weekend. It's fun when I ⁶_____ my friends in races, though!
(*beat / go out / represent / take part*)

I love football! I ⁷_____ my local team and I go to all their games. Last year, the club ⁸_____ a competition to find the most loyal fan, and I was in the top ten! I sometimes play football with my friends, but I've never ⁹_____ a goal!
(*hold / score / support / take up*)

2 Complete the crossword.

```
        ¹C
  ²O □ □ □ □ □ □
        │
   ³S │ P □ □ □ □ □
        │
      ⁴T □ □ □ □ □ □
        │
 ⁵S □ □ □ □ □ □ □
        │
      O
        │
 ⁶R □ □ □ □ □
```

Across
2 the people you play against in a sport
3 people who watch a team and want them to win
4 the people you play in a game or competition with
5 someone who watches a sports event live, in a stadium
6 the person who decides if players are following the rules

Down
1 someone who takes part in a competition

3 Complete what the people say with *do*, *play* or *go*.

★ HAVE YOUR SAY
What's your sporting dream?

I'd like to ¹_____ running in the desert – what a challenge! **Emma, 16**

I'd like to be fit enough to climb a mountain and then ²_____ a workout at the top! **Erica, 15**

I want to ³_____ ice skating on a frozen lake in Canada – cool! **Stella, 16**

I'd love to ⁴_____ basketball with one of the great American teams – but I'll never be tall enough! **Paul, 15**

I'd like to ⁵_____ yoga on an empty beach in the Caribbean – just me, the sea and the sand! **Rose, 15**

Tennis is my favourite sport, so of course my dream is to ⁶_____ tennis at Wimbledon! **Matt, 14**

I'd love to ⁷_____ karate at a high level – cut through wood with my hands, that kind of thing! **Connor, 15**

4 Complete the quiz with the words in the box. Then do the quiz and check your answers on page 59.

course	court	rink	pitch	pool	ramp	track

SPORTS TRIVIA – test your knowledge!

1 The biggest natural ice skating _____ is the Rideau Canal in *Canada / Russia*. It is 7.8 km long.
2 The most footballs you can get on a football _____ is over *50,000 / 150,000*!
3 The deepest swimming _____ is in Italy and is *32 / 42* metres deep. It is used for diving.
4 The oldest ball boy to collect balls on a tennis _____ during an official match was *82 / 92*.
5 The oldest golf _____ in the world is in *the USA / Scotland*, where the sport started.
6 Yiannis Kouros holds the record for the longest distance that anyone has run on an athletics _____ in 24 hours. In 1997, Yiannis ran *202 / 303* km.
7 The fastest speed anyone has ever done on a skateboard wasn't on a skateboard _____, but on the road. The speed is *146 / 166* kilometres an hour.

GRAMMAR

1 Complete the sentences with the gerund form of the verbs in the box.

buy	climb	dive	run
join	meet	practise	spend

1 _____ to the top of a really high mountain must be an amazing experience!

2 I love _____ time with my cousins – we always have a laugh together.

3 I fancy _____ a sports club, but I'm not sure which sport to choose.

4 If you want to become good at any sport, you need to keep _____!

5 My uncle is mad about _____ – he does five km every morning!

6 I've never tried _____ because I hate being under water.

7 It's worth _____ a ticket to a professional football match if you love the sport.

8 My brother is keen on _____ other people who want to play chess.

2 Complete the sentences. Use *to* and the infinitive.

1 I think it _____ (be / important / do) exercise every day.

2 Maria _____ (learn / swim) last year.

3 I _____ (can't wait / take part) in my first judo competition.

4 Sasha loves music and she _____ (want / try) salsa dancing.

5 We were losing 2–0, but we finally _____ (manage / win) 3–2.

6 Hello. It _____ (be / nice / meet) you.

7 Last week, Sam _____ (persuade / me / go) skateboarding with him.

8 I'm often stressed, so I _____ (do / yoga / relax) in the evenings.

9 Max won two tickets for the cup final, so he _____ (invite / me / go) with him.

10 I needed a new belt, so I _____ (go / into town / buy) one.

3 Complete the text with the verbs in brackets. Use the gerund or *to* and the infinitive.

DO SOMETHING DIFFERENT!

1 _____ (spend) time on or near water is always fun, and most people enjoy 2 _____ (try) new sports. So why not have a go at wakeboarding? Wakeboarding is like skateboarding, only on water. There are plenty of places where you can do it, so you can look online 3 _____ (find) a place near you. We advise people 4 _____ (have) a few lessons so they can learn the basic skills. It's possible 5 _____ (hire) a board at first, but it's worth 6 _____ (buy) your own board as you get better, so you can practise 7 _____ (do) more difficult moves. Wakeboarding can be dangerous, so it's important 8 _____ (wear) a helmet. We also recommend 9 _____ (wear) a wetsuit 10 _____ (keep) you warm.

LISTENING PART 3

 19 For each question, write the correct answer in the gap.

Write one or two words or a number or a date or a time.

You will hear a gym owner called Lee Norton talking about a spin class.

New Spin Class with VR (Virtual Reality)

Lee's gym introduced the VR spin class in **(1)** _____.

Lee says the new VR spin class mixes exercise with **(2)** _____.

When Lee tried the class himself, he found exercising less **(3)** _____.

Lee says he most enjoys the VR session involving cycling through the **(4)** _____.

The best class for beginners is **(5)** _____ long.

Lee has plans for a VR class which offers the experience of **(6)** _____.

1 Read the article. Choose the best summary.

A Joe Fuller still loves surfing in spite of a terrible experience.

B Joe Fuller explains why surfing is an ideal sport for anyone who enjoys excitement and danger.

C Joe Fuller encourages other surfers to learn from his experience and be more careful.

2 Read the article again. Decide if the sentences are true or false. Correct the false sentences.

1 Joe started surfing as soon as he moved to the coast.

2 Joe says he loves surfing mainly because of how he feels when it goes well.

3 When Joe was carried out to sea, he wasn't sure what he should do.

4 Joe felt grateful when he was rescued, but also disappointed about losing his surfboard.

5 Joe had no fears about surfing again after his accident.

PUSH YOURSELF / B2

Choose the correct words to complete the comments about Joe's story.

sporty_jill
Wow! What an amazing story. It really cheered me **1**up / out to read about how brave Joe is! I think he should definitely stick **2**for / at his surfing and enjoy it!

dunc_rose
Reading about Joe made me want to **3**take / have a go at surfing myself, though I'm sure I won't **4**learn / pick it up very quickly!

seeseaemily
I **5**got / made into surfing a few years ago. I love it, but reading Joe's story has made me wonder if I should just chill **6**up / out on the beach instead, where it's safe!

andy_surf
Great story! Surfing is an amazing sport, once you **7**get / take the hang of it. It's a great way to wind **8**down / off when you're stressed. Yes, it can be dangerous, and that's why beginners should never go out surfing on their own. Hope you're reading this, Joe!

HOME **STORIES** ABOUT

MAD ABOUT SURFING

Joe Fuller can still clearly remember the first day he tried surfing. He was 14 years old. He'd moved to the coast two years before but wasn't very interested in sport at that time. Then some of his friends suggested going surfing one day in the summer holidays and he said yes. And that was it – he fell in love with the sport!

Joe says it's hard to describe what he thinks is so special about surfing. Obviously, it's wonderful to see the way the sea changes each day, so there are always new challenges to try. But according to Joe, the best thing is the amazing sense of freedom that you get when you're riding the perfect wave! But last year Joe had a terrifying experience. While he was surfing alone, the waves carried him out to sea, instead of bringing him back to the shore. Joe knew that it might be some time before rescuers found him, and

he knew the dangers of being in cold water for too long. But he also knew he had no choice but to stay with his surfboard and wait. Rescuers found him 16 hours later, nearly 20 kilometres away from the coast! He was cold and hungry, but still alive!

Joe says he can remember the mixture of feelings he had after he was rescued. He was exhausted, of course, and also quite upset that there wasn't room in the rescue helicopter to bring his surfboard with him! But most of all he couldn't wait to thank all the people who had worked so hard to find him and save his life.

And how did he feel about surfing again after his accident? He admits that he was a little nervous about getting into the water again, but once he rode his first wave the old excitement came back and he knew that stopping just wasn't an option!

SPEAKING

1 Choose the correct words to complete the sentences.

1 I love rugby, *so / since* I watch a lot of rugby matches on TV.

2 I live near the sea, *because / which is why* it's easy for me to do water sports.

3 *So / Because* I'm quite a sociable person, I prefer team sports to individual sports.

4 I'm going to watch an athletics competition on Saturday, *since / so* I'm a big fan of athletics.

5 *As / So* I don't have much money, I can't afford to join a gym.

6 I love tennis *which is why / because* it's a really exciting sport.

2 Two people are discussing the idea of building a gym. Complete the mini-dialogues with the correct words. There are two words you don't need.

agree	am	do	don't	how	really	right
should	sure	that's	think	what's		

A: I think it would be good idea to build a gym in the town. **1**_____ your opinion?

B: I **2**_____ with you. A gym would be a great idea.

A: I think they **3**_____ open a café at the gym. What **4**_____ you think?

B: Yes, you're **5**_____. I think **6**_____ a good idea.

A: **7**_____ about an outdoor gym in the park?

B: **8**_____? I'm not **9**_____ that's the best idea.

A: I think that most gyms are too expensive.

B: I **10**_____ agree with you. Some gyms are quite cheap, especially for students.

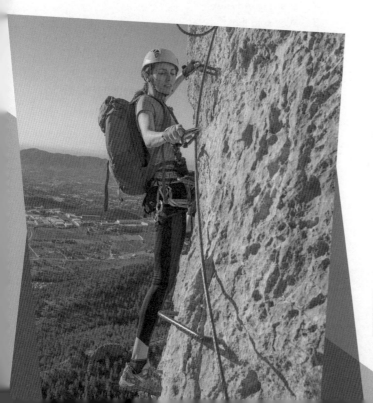

WRITING

1 Read the article about someone's favourite sport. Choose the best topic sentence for each paragraph. There is one topic sentence you don't need.

A I first started climbing five years ago. _____

B Some of my friends think that climbing is too dangerous. _____

C My favourite sport is climbing. _____

D Climbing can be done by people of any age. _____

1 It's a popular sport all over the world. Some people climb high mountains with ropes to keep them safe. Other people prefer low climbing with no ropes. You can also practise the sport in some climbing gyms.

2 Some friends invited me to go to the climbing gym with them. I enjoyed it, so I decided to take it up. Since then, I've joined a climbing club and next year I'm going climbing in France with the club.

3 Young children can start from the age of four or five, and people can continue climbing when they're quite old. In fact, climbing is a very good way to stay fit and strong all through your life. Climbing is a great sport for everyone!

2 Choose the correct linkers in the sentences.

1 Tennis is a fun sport to play. It's *too / also* a very exciting sport to watch.

2 I love singing *but / because* it always makes me feel cheerful.

3 I play *both / and* the guitar and the piano.

4 Last summer I went to some drama workshops, *which / and* I enjoyed a lot.

5 Dancing is a great way to keep fit. It's really good fun *too / also*.

6 I love acting, *but / because* I always get really nervous before a show.

3 Correct one spelling error in each sentence.

1 They forgot to bring there sports kit with them. _____

2 I love painting and I think its an amazing hobby. _____

3 I don't no where the swimming pool is. _____

4 There are a lot of sports facilities hear. _____

5 When you're watching birds, you have to be very quite and not make any noise. _____

6 You don't have to by a lot of equipment to play football. _____

14 ON TOP OF THE WORLD

VOCABULARY

1 **Choose the correct adjectives.**

1 I was really *disappointed / delighted* when my team lost the game.

2 We were all really *amused / shocked* when we saw how much damage the storm had done.

3 I always get really *satisfied / nervous* before exams.

4 I think we should do something to make Emma laugh. She looks really *miserable / impressed*!

5 It's important to talk to someone about your problems if you feel *depressed / jealous*.

2 **Complete the blog post with the words in the box.**

cheerful embarrassed guilty impressed jealous

DO YOUR FEELINGS EVER ANNOY YOU?

Mine do. For example, when a friend has done really well I want to feel pleased for him, and ¹_____ with his achievement, but I can't help feeling just a little bit ²_____ of his success. Or when I see someone slip on the ice, sometimes I can't help laughing and then I feel really ³_____ because it's wrong to be mean! Or I might do something silly when other people are watching, so I feel really ⁴_____ and it spoils my ⁵_____ mood. Wouldn't it be great if we could control our feelings?

3 **Read the descriptions of four people and choose two adjectives to complete each one.**

1 Matt's often _____ to people and he treats animals badly too. He can be quite _____ to his dog. (*cute / cruel / patient / rude*)

2 Conor never thinks before he does things, so he does some really _____ things, but he's really kind and _____ – he always buys me nice presents! (*cute / fashionable / generous / stupid*)

3 Your little sister has lovely big eyes – she's so _____! I love her long, _____ hair, too! (*clear / curly / cute / stupid*)

4 Reece is really _____ – he's never afraid to try new things, even if they're a bit dangerous. He's also very _____ with his annoying little sister! (*brave / stupid / patient / rude*)

GRAMMAR

1 **Complete the conditional sentences with the correct form of the verbs in brackets.**

1 Dan is always in a bad mood if he _____ (lose) at computer games.

2 If you are rude to Sam, he _____ (not invite) you to his party!

3 If Alice wasn't such a difficult person, more people _____ (like) her.

4 I'd be delighted if I _____ (get) 90% in a maths test!

5 I'll call you if I _____ (manage) to get tickets.

2 **Report the conversations.**

Adam: Where are you going?
Lia: I'm going home.
1 Adam asked Lia _____ .
2 Lia said that she _____ home.

Ella: Have you finished your project?
Paul: No, but I want to finish it by Friday.
3 Ella asked Paul _____ .
4 Paul said no, but he _____ by Friday.

Ana: Why did Emma leave the party?
Amy: I don't know.
5 Ana asked Amy why _____ .
6 Amy said that she _____ .

Laura: Is Tom OK?
Alex: I'm not sure. I'll talk to him.
7 Laura asked Alex _____ .
8 Alex said that he _____ sure, and he said he _____ to him.

3 **Complete the relative clauses in the joined sentences. Use *who, which, where* or *whose*.**

1 It's important to thank people. They help you.
It's important to thank people _____ .

2 Jen showed me the house. She grew up there.
Jen showed me the house _____ .

3 Tyler has offered to help with the food for the party. His dad is a chef.
Tyler, _____ , has offered to help with the food for the party.

4 The hotel was huge. We stayed in it.
The hotel _____ .

5 I passed the exam. I was delighted about it.
I passed the exam, _____ about.

4 Choose the correct modal verbs.

Teen Talk

GOT A PROBLEM?
Maybe we can help!

I feel tired all the time and I **¹can't / couldn't / shouldn't** stay awake at school. I know I **²must / ought / should** to get to bed earlier, but I keep getting messages from friends! **Lydia, 15**

Teen Talk's advice: You definitely **³should / need / might** get more sleep. If you're too tired, your brain isn't **⁴able / allowed / let** to work properly. We know it **⁵should / can't / must** be difficult for you, but remember, you really **⁶need to / must / don't have to** answer messages immediately! You **⁷can / can't / might** find it useful to leave your phone in the kitchen overnight.

My parents won't **⁸let / allow / make** me go out with my friends at the weekend. They say I **⁹must / could / have** to help with our family restaurant. We keep arguing about it. What can I do? **Dean, 16**

Teen Talk's advice: Talk to them calmly and explain that you are almost an adult and they **¹⁰shouldn't / can't / need to** give you a bit more freedom.

READING

Read the article. Choose the correct answers.

1 According to the writer,
  A we often experience more than one feeling in the same moment.
  B words are often more complicated than feelings.

2 In paragraph 2, the writer says that
  A there are too many different words for feelings.
  B sometimes words for feelings may be missing in our language.

3 You feel *myötähäpeä*
  A when you feel bad because you have done something foolish.
  B when you feel bad for another person.

4 *Iktsuarpok* is a feeling you get
  A when you are waiting for something bad to happen.
  B when you are looking forward to something.

5 Computers can already
  A help people to communicate through their minds.
  B see and understand people's feelings.

6 According to the writer, in the future
  A computers may help us to put our feelings into words.
  B we may not need to use words to communicate our feelings.

FEELINGS WITHOUT WORDS?

When someone asks you how you're feeling, do you sometimes find it hard to choose the right word to explain? That's not surprising, because feelings are complicated things, and the words we use to describe them often seem too simple. For example, how do you feel when you fail an exam or lose a sports competition? Disappointed? Angry? Embarrassed? Scared? The chances are, you feel all of these things at the same time and there's no word that *really* describes what's going on in your head.

People have always found it difficult to put feelings into words, and sometimes what you're feeling may not even have a word in your language. There are lots of different words for feelings in different languages, like the Finnish word *myötähäpeä*, for example. This describes the feeling you get when you see someone else doing something silly, and you feel embarrassed for them! Or there's the Danish word *hygge*, which means that lovely warm feeling you get when you sit around the fire with good friends on a cold winter's evening. Or what about the Inuit word *iktsuarpok,* which is that feeling of excitement you get when you're expecting someone to arrive at your house, and you can't stop looking out of the window to see if they're coming. We recognise all these feelings, but of course it's hard to explain them if our own language doesn't have a word for them.

In the future, however, things might become easier. Scientists are working on computer systems that can 'read' people's thoughts. The computer 'watches' the electrical activity in someone's brain and then changes this into a digital message, which can be sent to another person. Scientists in Spain have already managed to send the thought 'hello' from one brain to another in this way. So, it's possible that in the future, when someone asks you how you're feeling, you might be able to turn a switch so that they can feel exactly what you're feeling, with no need to put it into words!

Complete the sentences with compound adjectives formed from the words in brackets.

1 There are nine _____ students in my class. (blue / eyes)

2 Joe's dad is a _____ artist. (respect / highly)

3 She's now got a very _____ job. (pay / well)

4 My grandad may be old, but he's still very _____. (open / mind)

5 I saw an old photo of my dad when he was a _____ student! (long / hair)

6 This is a _____ film, so we should go and see it. (recommend / highly)

LISTENING PART 4

 20 **For each question, choose the correct answer.**

You will hear an interview with a musician called Molly Ford talking about growing up with famous parents.

1 Molly first realised her parents were famous when
  A her family were followed by photographers.
  B she saw her parents' picture in a magazine.
  C fans stopped her parents in the street.

2 Although Molly enjoyed going on tour with her parents, she missed
  A her friends.
  B her daily routine.
  C her room at home.

3 How did Molly feel when she read articles about her parents?
  A angry because they said unpleasant things
  B pleased because she was mentioned in them
  C proud because so many people liked her parents

4 Molly remembers her parents often telling her that being famous
  A can have several advantages.
  B is never a permanent situation.
  C prevents you from having a normal life.

5 What does Molly say about her parents' famous friends?
  A They tell her lots of things about their lives.
  B They are just normal people to her.
  C They act differently in private and in public.

6 Molly think that if she has children in the future, she will
  A give up performing.
  B go travelling with them.
  C ask her parents to look after them.

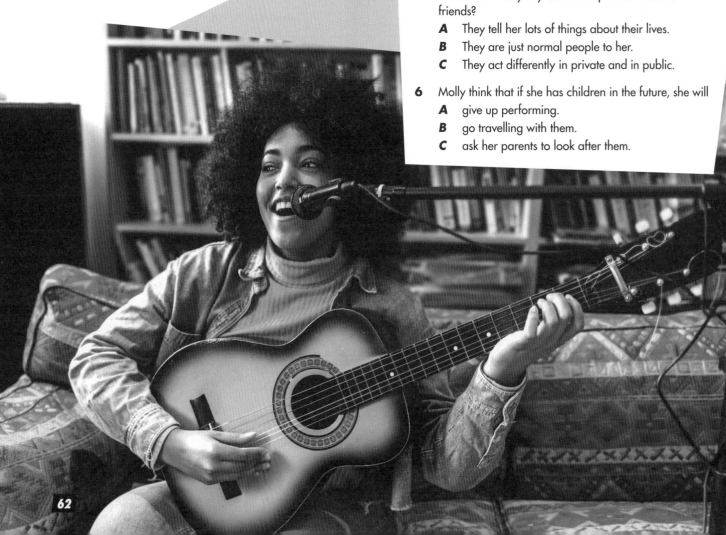

SPEAKING

1 Complete the questions with the words in the box.

> can   do   how   is   long
> often   which   why

1 .... do you usually get to school?
2 .... you swim?
3 How .... do you go shopping?
4 .... you prefer to play sport or watch it?
5 How .... have you known your best friend?
6 .... it important to do exercise every week?
7 .... do you enjoy going on holiday?
8 .... is more fun, going to the cinema or watching a movie at home?

2 Choose the best answer to each question in exercise 1.

1 **A** I sometimes walk, or I get the bus if I'm late.
  B I usually get to school at half past eight.

2 **A** No, I don't like swimming in the sea, but I like going to the swimming pool.
  B Yes, I can. I'm quite a good swimmer.

3 **A** I usually go with my friends because they help me to choose new clothes.
  B I don't go every week, but I go about once a month.

4 **A** I'm quite sporty, so I prefer to play sports myself.
  B I like football and tennis, and I often watch them on TV.

5 **A** His name is James, and he's 15 years old, like me.
  B I first met him when I was five, so I've known him for about 10 years.

6 **A** I think it's very important to do regular exercise, to keep fit and healthy.
  B I go running every week because I think it's a good kind of exercise.

7 **A** I like it because when I'm on holiday I feel completely relaxed.
  B I usually go to the beach and lie in the sun or swim in the sea.

8 **A** I often watch movies with my friends at home because we all like the same kinds of movies.
  B I prefer to go to the cinema because films look more exciting on a big screen.

WRITING

1 Look at the student's paragraph plan for a profile of a friend. Then read sentences A–H and decide which two sentences should go in each paragraph (1–4).

> ## Profile of Lily
>
> 1 her life and family   ....
> 2 her appearance   ....
> 3 her personality   ....
> 4 things we do together   ....

A She's very kind and friendly, and loves meeting new people.
B We sometimes watch films or play computer games together.
C She's quite tall, and she's got fair, curly hair.
D Lily is my cousin and she lives in Amsterdam.
E Usually when we get together we just chat for hours!
F She loves clothes, so she always wears smart, fashionable clothes.
G She's also very intelligent and she wants to study medicine at university.
H Her family moved there when she was three.

2 Read another student's profile of a friend. Choose the correct words to complete it.

Sarah is my best friend. She was born in France, ¹but / when she moved to London with her family when she was seven years old. Now she goes to the same school as me, ²so / because I see her every day.
³Although / However Sarah and I go to the same school, we are very different. Sarah has short, fair hair and wears very fashionable clothes. She's ⁴too / also very intelligent, and she wants to study business at university.
⁵However / So, Sarah doesn't only think about herself and her career. She's very kind and generous, and she loves doing things to help other people.
We always have fun ⁶because / when we meet up. Sometimes we cook a meal together, ⁷as well / or we watch a film and then talk about it afterwards. I love talking to Sarah ⁸because / so she always has something interesting to say!

ACKNOWLEDGEMENTS

The authors and publishers acknowledge the following sources of copyright material and are grateful for the permissions granted. While every effort has been made, it has not always been possible to identify the sources of all the material used, or to trace all copyright holders. If any omissions are brought to our notice, we will be happy to include the appropriate acknowledgements on reprinting and in the next update to the digital edition, as applicable.

Key: ST = Starter, U = Unit

Text

U2: Guardian News and Media Limited for the text from 'How Marvel's superheroes found the magic to make us all true believers' by Jeffrey A Brown, *The Guardian*, 31/08/2013. Copyright Guardian News & Media Ltd 2013.

Photography

The following images are sourced from Getty Images.

UST: Klaus Vedfelt/DigitalVision; Jetta Productions Inc./DigitalVision; Robin Skjoldborg/Cultura; Nikada/E+; monkeybusinessimages/iStock/Getty Images Plus; andresr/E+; **U1:** Holger Leue/Lonely Planet Images; Leland Bobbe/Stockbyte; Westend61; Eva-Katalin/E+; Daniel Schoenen/Look; Art Wager/E+; **U2:** Hulton Archive/Moviepix; Pekic/E+; **U3:** guruxoox/iStock/Getty Images Plus; LauriPatterson/E+; Monty Rakusen/Cultura; Trevor Williams/DigitalVision; Image Source; **U4:** Visions of our Land/Photolibrary; RosLol/Moment; Hill Street Studios LLC/DigitalVision; **U5:** Hero Images; pixelfit/E+; Paul Bradbury/OJO Images; **U6:** vgajic/E+; Caiaimage/Sam Edwards; Tim Robberts/Taxi; **U7:** Luca Sage/Taxi; Ridofranz/iStock/Getty Images Plus; **U8:** Pierre-Yves Babelon/Moment; Johner Images; Kai-Otto Melau/Getty Images Sport; **U9:** LongHa2006/E+; Colin Hawkins/The Image Bank; Astrakan Images/Cultura; **U10:** Elena Odareeva/iStock Editorial/Getty Images Plus; Ashley Cooper/Corbis NX; SolStock/E+; Tuayai/iStock/Getty Images Plus; Westend61; **U11:** Jon Bower at Apexphotos/Moment Open; View Pictures/Universal Images Group; Eva-Katalin/E+; Westend61; TonTectonix/iStock/Getty Images Plus; **U13:** Manchan/DigitalVision; ranplett/E+; ianmcdonnell/E+; Alfredo Maiquez/Lonely Planet Images; **U14:** Nick Daly/Cultura; Vladimir Vladimirov/E+; Caiaimage/Chris Ryan/OJO+.

The following images are sourced from other sources/libraries

U2: Serhii Bobyk/Alamy Stock Photo; **U12:** ZUMA Press, Inc./Alamy Stock Photo.

Front cover photography by Supawat Punnanon/EyeEm; Patrick Foto; fStop Images-Caspar Benson.

Illustrations

Chris Chalik

Audio

Produced by Ian Harker and recorded at The SoundHouse Studios, London

Page make up

EMC Design Ltd